THE MOONCAVE MYSTERY

THE MOONCAVE MYSTERY

ROBERT K. LEŚNIAKIEWICZ

MILOŠ JESENSKÝ

***

Originally published in Poland by Studio Wydawnicze "Za Prog" in 2004 as Tajemnica Ksiezycowj Jaskini

***

***

Paperback ISBN: 978-1-7342857-8-9
ePub ISBN: 978-1-3936355-9-8

***

Written by Robert Konstanty Leśniakiewicz & Dr Miloš Jesenský
Published by Royal Hawaiian Press
Cover art by Tyrone Roshantha
Translated by Szymon Nowak
Publishing Assistance: Balasubramanian Nambi

***

For more works by this author, please visit:
www.royalhawaiianpress.com

***

Version Number 1.00

TABLE OF CONTENTS

An exotic legend or truth - Sebastian Berzeviczy enters the stage - Pastor Bucholtz's testimony - Who was the Spanish *Securitate* looking for?

CHAPTER 5 - Dispute over Dr. Horák's identity 50

How it all began: adventurers, researchers and ministerial officials - *You are wanted, Captain Horak.* - Exploration in the field - Information from Eduard Piovarče - Moon Cave as part of the intelligence game?

CHAPTER 6 - New search horizons 63

Nota spaelologica - More questions than answers - Again Belianske Tatras? - From the research journal of Walter Pavliš and Ivo Hlásenský - Letter from Piotr Parahuz - Searching in insurgent history: false twins and secret Nazi research - Dr. Horák really existed.

CHAPTER 7 - From Nazi scholars to NKVD agents 84

A small encouragement to start with: a strange photograph of Robert - *Retaliation weapons* under Diablak - Christmas Eve in Luboń - What did the tank wreck hide? - Interview with a witness of those days - Views of Maciej Kuczyński and two reports on underground spaces.

CHAPTER 8 - Secret of the Orava Beskids 101

Strange phenomena over Magura and mysterious lights on the slopes - Bottomless pit, missing people, thunders without a storm for the second time - Arrivals from the night sky - About the meteorite transformed into hoes and plowshares - The topic returns: Strange discovery on Červené vrchy.

INTRODUCTION

The Levoča Mountains, Slovakia
Today

The boy took one last look at the blackthorn slope bathed in the light of summer morning and then entered the dark expanse of the cave hole hidden behind the rocking snowmen under the tall montane spruces. There was little light here, and he couldn't form his opinion about what surrounded him. In his imagination, the caves consisted of underground halls and corridors full of wonders, marble mushrooms stuck to the walls, with a tire of underground raindrops - stalactites, stalagmites, and stalagnates created by millions of years of water work and other wonders of the underground world. Meanwhile, here, against his expectations, was a dark smooth chamber narrowing into the corridor.

He took a deep breath and plunged into darkness and silence. Bits of burnt wood and branches from the old fire crackled under his sneakers and something round and smooth like a ball protruded a little further from the clay floor. He overcame fear and sighed again, and the cave answered him with reverberations and a sinister echo lost somewhere in its depths. That round thing was the human skull of some nameless Wehrmacht soldier, which he recognized by the characteristic shape of the helmet and whose body probably turned to dust after decades. But that wasn't the thing he feared the most.

The boy heard only silence and had the impression that this silence was an unspeakable threat to him. Despite the thick darkness, he felt as if the shadows of long-dead soldiers had been coming out of the walls and stretching their skeletal hands towards him. The helmet fell out of his hand and rolled rattling down the cave floor. The boy, in a panic, didn't even try to lift it, but turned and ran toward the cave's opening, in which particles of dust danced in the rays of the sun.

As he emerged from the tufts of grass and sharp rock teeth surrounding the entrance, he heard the call of his brother, who in the meantime was digging with a survival shovel in a small excavation. When he came closer to the excavation – in the bright light of the July sun *this thing* was not so terrible, as if "there" – in the darkness of the cave, hidden under the rocks and spruce roots, had been a cut part of a human skull, several bones, and shoe remains. Also, among the remains, was a military cap, a rusty badge of the insurgent army.

"We have a problem," said the older boy, putting a rusty piece of metal in the pocket of his pants, in which he then wiped his hands soiled with clay. "Here," he waved his right hand wide toward the excavation where his brother stood, "can be some grenades or other explosives. We will need to call someone."

A few hours later, a patrol car of the sapper unit climbed the slope covered with small excavations, on which men walked in heavy explosion-proof suits with mine detectors in their hands. When they finished their work and found the place safe, their commander, who in the meantime checked the entrance to an unknown cave, talked for a long time with his supervisor over the field radio. In a short time, appeared Lada Nivas of the green military police, whose soldiers closed access to this area for all bystanders – including residents of nearby villages, nature protection guards, forest workers, and foresters.

What was also weird is that on the slope a small tent town was build, covered from the top with masking nets. There were satellite antennas, strong reflectors, monitoring equipment, field electricity generators, and so on and so forth. One hour before sunset, the amazed inhabitants of the surrounding villages, terrified and curious about passing motorcades of olive-green military trucks, had one more interesting show – a military helicopter emerged from the interior of the bloody setting sun, flown low over the roofs, and had disappeared over the mountain. None of them were close enough to see where the machine landed. They also didn't see a man in civilian clothes getting out of the helicopter, accompanied by people dressed in chemical protective suits and gas masks, with various instruments at their side.

"Let me report you," the man in uniform with the lieutenant colonel's distinctions said vigorously, "that we found it. We found the Moon Cave. This is how it would look like in a bad movie like "The X-Files" or something like that *made in Hollywood*. Above all, we will show the reader the chronological course of study and search for this artifact, which perhaps dates back to the time of the existence of Atlantis or even Atlantica."

The history of the search for the Moon Cave reminds meanders of Dymitriada or the history of life and achievements of such characters as **Copernicus, Retyk, Devius, Kelley, Sędziwoj, Dr. Faustus,** and other well-known figures of Polish and European history, which are characterized by this "elusiveness" characteristic of Polish and European Renaissance. Many people were looking for it, many gave up, but the engaging secret was disturbing, and still, people gave into its sinister charm. Also, at stake is not only the discovery of an amazing artifact but perhaps also new technologies or new information about the history of our planet.

Specialists, scholars, journalists, ufologists, historians, and outsider researchers like us, helped us in our search. It is impossible to name them all, so let us at least thank them all here and now, taking the opportunity which is publishing the book. Of course, special thanks to the publisher - **Mr. Pavel Mészáros.**

Thanks to him our second joint work, which is a contribution to the common European cultural heritage, saw the light of day. It is a continuation of the subject raised in our earlier works: "Bohové atomových válek" (Ústi nad Labem 1998) by Dr. Jesenský and my "Projekt Tatry" (Cracow 2002). Now, let's examine some facts.

CHAPTER 1

Records of Captain Horák

Jacques Bergier's account - An unusual story of an insurgent captain - Dr. Horák finds a strange cave - Chronicle of extraordinary events day after day - Traces of Atlantis in Slovakia?

We would like to present to the reader the state of our knowledge about one of the most interesting mysteries of our planet and the history of civilizations that exist on it. One of them is the Metal Walls Well, discovered by a Slovak fighter during the Slovak National Uprising at the end of 1944. In addition, we present our assumptions of the conclusions that may arise after reading this material.

We present the reader materials in a chronological manner that we have developed ourselves and which we received from our friends from Slovakia, Poland, the Czech Republic, and the United States, and for which we thank them very much. Here is the first of them - an article by **Miloš Jesenský**, published in "Wizje Peryferyjne" No. 2, 1996.

Slovaks and Czechs call it POLMESIAČNA JASKYNA, or just as in the title – MESIAČNA JASKYNA, which means the Crescent or Moon Cave. In world literature, it is most often called - the Metal Walls Cave or simply, the Well, which is imprecise because it is more a shaft, a steep excavation, and not a natural formation, such as a cave or grot. According to all researchers and enthusiasts of hypotheses about the existence of ancient civilizations or extraterrestrial civilizations, the Moon Cave is a trail and evidence that about 20,000 years ago in the territory of today's Central Europe, there was a civilization of the Hyperborean Era, so accurately and visually described by **Robert E. Howard**, or there was landing of representatives of "another civilization" unearthly (e.g. Shamballa, Agatha, underground K'n-yan or from the legendary island of Atlantis) or extraterrestrial. In Poland, the topic related to these peculiarities, as there are many similar shafts around the world, is rather unknown. If you are interested, please refer to **Thomas de Jean's** "Księga Tajemnic 2" published in Łódź in 1992, where the text about the Moon Cave is on pages 79-88. Competent Tatra guides and many hunters of singularity treat the Moon Cave only as a legend with no factual fortitude. The thing is that to date, no one has managed to find the place that **Antonin T. Horák** writes about in his diary, and this is the only source with a description of the Moon Cave. In 1992-95, a Slovak researcher, medic, and ufologist, Dr. Miloš Jesenský, investigated this matter and gave us the results of his search; so, we now have the opportunity to present the results of his work.

At one time, **Ronald D. Calais** told the world about the discovery, in the late 1960s, in the quarries in McDermott (Ohio, USA) at a depth of about 15 meters, of a prehistoric shaft of circular cross-section. Nobody had noticed it before, and the people working in the quarries buried it with production waste, small stones, and gravel.

The events I write about further are presented in a diary by the late Capt. Dr. Antonin T. Horák, from where the entire text was quoted almost literally in the National Speleological Society Bulletin - "NSS News" No. 3,1965, from where it was reprinted in the work of **Jacques Bergier** and the INFO group, "Le livre de l'inexplicable," in Paris, 1972. The author of the diary, a former officer of the insurgent army formed during the Slovak National Uprising and then a linguist, tries to encourage speleologists to find what Jacques Bergier called "the strangest puzzle of our planet" - the old shaft of a prehistoric mine, which he discovered in one of caves in Slovakia. Here is how Antonin T. Horák described it. He is the author of the account that caused all the commotion around the Moon Cave (Bergier J. Et al. : Le livre de l´inexplicable, Albin Michel, Paris 1972, Czech ed. Ivo Železný, Praha 1995, p. 38-49. *Parts of the text that have been left out in French translation are marked in bold*).

October 23, 1944

Yesterday, in the early morning, we were found by Slavek while we were hidden in this cave. Today at dusk, he returned to us with his daughter Hanka and brought food and medicine. We had nothing in our mouths since Friday, and before that, during the last two skirmishes, we only ate cornbread, and that was not enough.

On Saturday afternoon, the remnants of our battalion (184 soldiers and officers, 1/4 of whom were wounded, and 16 people were carried on stretchers) hobbled on the snow on the northern slope. My company was in the rearguard. On Sunday at dawn, we were attacked from a distance of 300 meters by two 70-millimeter guns. We resisted for 12 hours, then repelled the attack, but the left-wing couldn't withstand, which cost us several wounds. During the fight with the enemy, I was wounded by a bayonet and a bullet in my left hand, and in addition, I was wounded in the head, which happened in the next battle. Due to the lack of a helmet, I was hit hard on the head - hence the nagging wound.

I regained consciousness when someone pulled me out of the trench. He was a tall peasant. He rubbed my hands and head with snow and smiled. Then this Good Samaritan helped Jurek. He took off his pants, pulled a splinter from his leg and put it on the snow. He skillfully dressed a deep wound on Martin's stomach. When he made a makeshift stretcher, he introduced himself to us as a herdsman (actually a senior shepherd) Slavek, to whom the pastures surrounding us belonged. We got to our shelter with his help after 4 hours.

Slavek threw several boulders and showed a narrow hole – the entrance to the spatial cave. He put Martin to the corner and hid him, he also hid us and the cave, and then bowing, he also hid himself in front of the back wall, where the entrance to its further part was visible.

When he was leaving us, he repeated the same ritual and asked me not to go deeper into the cave. I followed him a bit, saying I would gather something to eat. He told me that he was in this cave together with his father and grandfather, that this is a vast labyrinth full of abyss which they never wanted to explore or visit, that there are poisonous gases, and "it's haunted." I returned to the cave around midnight completely exhausted. I relieved my headache with snow. Martin was unconscious and Jurek had a fever. We ate a modest supper. I put hot stones on Martin, and Jurek took the first watch.

It was a horrible night. When Martin returned to consciousness, I gave him three aspirins and some water with plum brandy, exactly ten drops. Hungry, Jurek wandered around two German helmets, where snow water boiled, to which I added ten drops of plum brandy. Perhaps because of the snow flood and the avalanche threat, *as well as numerous enemy ski patrols that were wandering in the area*, Slavek won't come to us sooner than in a few days. With two sick people on my hands, I couldn't even try to hunt some animal, let alone, I could get lost in unknown terrain. We have a cave, to which, as Slavek said, there may be another entrance and it is possible that even an animal hibernated here. I considered these possibilities out loud, and Jurek chewed on fir bark and asked me to go deep into the cave to hunt. He promised me he wouldn't tell anyone. I didn't feel hungry, but I was interested in what could frighten so confident Slavek, that he was calling God. I took my gun and torch with me.

After an hour and a half, walking a fairly comfortable and safe corridor, I got into a long vestibule of sorts that ended with a small opening.

I went into this hole and bruised my knee. There was something similar to a large black silo sunk into the white ground, something like black lava covered in salt or ice. It disturbed me and I felt a strange fear because I realized that what I was looking at is the work of human hands. The shaft was curved as if a cylinder with a radius of 25 meters had been imprinted in it. In the place where the roller was in contact with the wall, white stalactites and stalagmites formed. The wall was blue and black, made of a material that was a combination of steel, glass, or porcelain and rubber. I touched the substance with a knife; I couldn't even scratch it. I thought I was in a wild land where there was nothing that civilization would have created and there is an artifact as high as a tower, like a castle tower sunk into the ground and covered with infiltrates – the cold went through my bones due to all this.

There was a narrow and long crack in the wall, at the bottom about 20-25 cm wide, at the very top barely 2-5 cm, through which a person barely would be able to squeeze. Its interior is completely black and covered with sharp jags, as big as a fist. The bottom of the crevice had the shape of a shallow trough in YELLOW SANDSTONE and is inclined at an angle of about 60°. I inserted a lit torch there, it hissed like coals thrown into the water and went out.

I wanted to examine the item on the spot and found that I could squeeze through the gap. First, I pushed my head and right hand there. The hand with the candle also passed, but I had to act quickly because there was little stearin. I gave up but only for now because the mystery fascinated me. I decided to come back here again.

I returned to our cave around four in the afternoon. Jurek washed Martin and put him among warm stones. I gave him three aspirins and hot water with plum brandy. I explained to Jurek that I would need a twine, pole, and a torch to hunt. Fortunately, the Slavkovs came with supplies.

Then I went with them to collect brush for torches. I came back to the cave about two in the morning half-dead from tiredness – but at last, we ate our fill, Jurek even too much – so I took the second watch.

October 24, 1944

The night went quietly. Martin drank an herbal decoction with honey to fight the fever. I hope that he will recover. Jurek no longer had such a swollen back, but my head was still not right. I cut our belts and thongs, so I gained about 8 meters of strong rope. At 10 o'clock I was again at the wall, where I used the rod with a tied rope, after which I passed to the other side of the dark shaft crack. This time I had a carbide lamp, which I threw there first. I didn't see anything but heard something like the sound of flowing water. I was afraid that there would be a chasm behind the gap and that I would fall headfirst. There were no loose stones in the gap, so I broke off a few stalagmites and threw them into the dark. I could hear them rolling down the floor and stopping with a crash, which made me sure that there was a bottom there. I dropped the burning torch and followed it. I flew out of the crack on the other side, rolled, and stopped on a wall that was as smooth as the one on the other side if the cave. The lamp was still burning next to me and I heard some strange sounds. When I lit the torches, I noticed that I was in a shaft with curved black walls that formed an almost vertical chimney with a sickle cross-section. I can't describe this darkness or the multiplied sound of my breath or every move. The bottom of the shaft was lined with (or carved in) solid limestone.

All the light I had was unable to accurately illuminate the ceiling, where the walls ended or touched. The horizontal distance between the walls of the shaft was about 8 meters, and between the "sickle spikes" as much as 25 meters. For further research, I needed more torches and longer poles, which, however, would not fit in the entrance gap.

I was coming back dirty but full of hope that I would be able to explore this extraordinary structure, which was probably the only one in the world. This time, I managed to break through the gap without any problems. I got out of the shaft, smoked, and went back to my companions in misery. On the way back I wanted to catch a bat but to no avail. Jurek cooked potatoes and forgave my failure in hunting, then anointed wounds on my back and sewed my shirt. Martin ate a piece of bread and washed it down with a decoction of herbs seasoned with honey. After 6 pm, I went to gather firewood and torches and returned around 10 pm. Jurek guarded the cave all the time.

October 25, 1944

The night passed peacefully. Martin is doing well. I'm also glad that Jurek's wounds are already healing and he would like to come with me. but it would be better if he did not know anything about the secret of the cave.

As before, I slipped into the slit after removing my clothes, but this time with my feet forward. Even though I tied torches to two poles, I couldn't see the shaft ceiling. I shot twice up the wall. It roared like a lightning strike, or rather it sounded like the roar of a passing express, and that was all. So, I fired one bullet at each wall once more. Blue and green sparks jumped from the hit places at a height of about 15 meters above me, and the bang was such that I had to cover my ears. When I hit the wall with the ice ax, I caused another wave of rumbling.

Then I probed the regolith at the bottom of the shaft and then started digging in the corners of the "crescent" where the limestone was the weakest. In the right corner was a dry loam, in the left corner under a half-meter layer of loam, I found the bones of a large animal. When I kept digging, after 150 cm, I found a smooth striation on the back wall, as if horizontal ripples, which seemed to be warmer than the rest of the rock. I examined these features with my ears, and I knew I was not mistaken. Under the loam, the bottom was quite hard.

When the torches burned, I felt cold sweat on me. I left the crescent shaft, dressed and went to the place where the bats were. I hunted seven of them. Jurek made a stew of bread, herbs and these bats. ***Slavek and Olga, his second daughter, came with the darkness and brought straw, hay, sheepskins, and healing herbs: blackthorn, sedum and iris seeds, which are excellent substitutes for coffee. Meanwhile, I looked for pine torches and two long poles and returned around midnight. I gave Martin water and other aspirins. Jurek guarded us all night again.***

October 26, 1944

The night passed peacefully. I came back to the shaft to continue my research. Again, despite my use of the longest pole and torch, I was unable to light the ceiling. I shot above the lit part - the bullets brought out huge blue-green sparks and rumbling from the wall but didn't chip off any crumbs of the strange wall covering. However, the projectiles made half-finger long scratches in the wall, from which a sharp smell came out. Again, I started digging in the left corner and found that the metal lining stretched deeper, which wasn't in the right corner.

I got out of the shaft and looked at the outer wall and its surroundings. There were several glass-like spots in the stalactite. When I scraped them, I received a very fine powder that couldn't be collected without glue. I decided to get glue from bat claws. I wanted to get at least a small sample of this material, from which the extremely smooth walls of the crescent shaft were made. Despite the fact that I always fired at the same place where the bullets bounced, I didn't get anything but the sharp smell and the vibrating sound of ricochet bullets.

On the way back, I caught a few bats and again we had them in a "stew." I told Jurek to cut off their legs. In the evening, as usual, Slavek and his daughter came and brought a quarter of a deer, half a kilo of salt, and a bag of carbide. Jurek was again on guard all night.

October 27, 1944

Martin died in his sleep. Jurek, who knew his family decided to hand over [to her] his belongings – a wallet with 643 crowns, a watch with an engraving, and a death certificate that I issued to him. Now, we could leave and join our battalion, which was located east of Košice. Jurek could go about 10 km a day, but we had to move carefully. We decided to leave the following day.

At 10 am, I was in the cave, and I was looking for a way to get to it from behind or from above. It didn't come across as if there were ice and poisonous gases in it, and I think they were not there, despite the Slavkovs' assurances. Then I crawled into the shaft, kept digging and thinking about this problem. I returned to the cave around 4 pm. I ordered Jurek to pack our things, clean the weapons, prepare food for seven days and hand everything we borrowed, back to Slavek. He came with both daughters as soon as he learned that Martin had died. We moved the deceased to the trench and buried him wrapped in blankets. *Slavek was to set up a decent cross there in the spring, for which I gave him 150 crowns. He was reporting to me the enemy's eastward movement as best he could. Jurek and I returned to the cave around midnight, and he again took both guards, for he could sleep well tomorrow.*

October 28, 1944

A quiet night and a good breakfast this time. I etched my name, etc. on the strap, and all this I put into the gold case of my watch, then put it into a bottle, which I clogged with a mixture of clay and charcoal. I put this proof of my stay in the "moon shaft" on the remains of burnt torches. It seems that it will stay there for a long time until the limestone infiltrates cover the entrance to the shaft completely. Slavek had no son to whom he could pass the secret of the shaft, his daughters didn't know it, and it's possible that they got married in other villages. If I don't return to this cave, it will disappear from human memory in a few decades.

I sat by the fire and wondered for what this structure with walls two meters thick and such a strange shape was to be used, but I didn't come up with anything. How deep was it stuck in the rock? Is there anything else besides this shaft? Was it a creation of human hands? How much is true of Plato's legends about long-lost civilizations possessing magical techniques that we cannot even imagine?

I'm a cautious man in judgment, with a university education, but I must admit that there, between these tall, perfectly sloping, almost mathematically accurate, curved walls, black and smooth as satin, was a breath of some unknown power. Now, I understood exactly the behavior of Slavek and his ancestors, who with their practical and simple minds saw some spells in it. Slavek hid the fact of the existence of the Moon Cave for fear of invading hordes of tourists and everything that such an invasion carries. Was he afraid of the commercialization of his simple life in the bosom of nature? When I come back here again, it will be with a team of experts bound by an oath of silence: geologists, metallurgists, speleologists, and even if this object is important for the development of science and our civilization, we will have to respect Slavek's views.

On my way back, I masked the holes leading to the cave. Perhaps it has some entrances that Slavek doesn't know, through which some "treasure" hunter or speleologist can enter. I came back at three in the afternoon. Around five, came the Slavkovs bringing several hard-boiled eggs. ***Jurek asked Slavek to talk face to face. Then Hanka said what was going on – namely that she wanted to marry him. She laughed and cried. Jurek gave her his picture and the gold watch his father had brought him from America. Jurek was a wealthy carpenter in Bratislava. I was invited to the wedding and hoped to attend. To convince them that I was serious about it, I gave Hanka a letter to my friend a jeweler, in which I told him to give her a druse of Czech garnets as a wedding present. Slavek brought their family Bible, and I made the appropriate entries in it.***

Saying goodbye in Slovak, we shook hands hard, took our weapons and belongings and went. When we entered the forest, we looked back and saw Slavek masking the entrance to the cave. His daughters were blurring our tracks. The snow was gleaming in the bright light of the rising moon.

October 30, 1944

We moved slowly because it was dark on summer paths. For several days, we camped in pine forests and listened to the roar of guns. We saw a group of insurgents who fought mountain shooters and blue fascist policemen. The fascists withdrew, and we joined the insurgents and were their guests all day. It was a mixed group from Hechaluts, ŻOB, and DROR from the Rzeszów Voivodeship in neighboring Poland. They helped our insurgents and couldn't return, due to the deep snow, to their operational area between Cracow and Przemyśl. Their doctor was Rachela W., a widow of a murdered Jewish doctor. She told us about the struggles of the group Jesia [Jasia] of Fryman Banda with the Nazis and fed us warm food twice. When these Jewish fighters went north, we had

to go south towards Košice, where we arrived on the sixth day. In Košice, we received the order to go to our unit, which was waiting for the offensive of the Red Army to join it until the end of the war.

In the last days of World War II, traveling to the Czech Republic, I visited this place again. The Slavkovs lived temporarily in Ždiar. I visited Martin's grave and went to see the entrance to the cave. I gave the teeth of the animal that I found there to a conservator in the department of the paleontological museum in Uzhgorod [Ukraine]. The conservator described them as the teeth of an adult cave bear (Ursus spealeus). Again, a question arose: the entrance is very narrow, how did this bear get there? After all, the block of limestone and stalactites were intact and there was no indication that anything damaged them. Is it possible that the bear fell into the shaft when it was still connected to the surface?

In the correspondence discussing the plans to publish this journal, Dr. George W. Moore is leaning toward the theory that the "moon shaft" could have arisen as a result of the dissolution of the limestone layer lying between parallel layers of the chert. I'm skeptical about this because the entire inner surface of the "moon shaft" is homogeneous. This hypothesis doesn't explain parallel grooving on the wall surface in the left corner.

On a recent visit to that area, I explored the entire mountainside above the cave and found no hole that could be connected to the "crescent shaft." However, in such young mountains as the Tatras, they could be blocked by some rock slip, which often happens there.

CHAPTER 2

Searching for the Moon Cave

Copper ore mine 12,000 years old? - *Dramatis personae* from the captain's journal - First searches and first doubts - Inaccurate geographical data - Cave found and lost again.

In the previous chapter, you read the information from Capt. Dr. Antonin Horák, in the conclusion of which we can read the hypothesis that the Moon Cave is an artifact left after civilization, which Plato described in his dialogues "Timajos" and "Critias." Personally, we are convinced that this is a remnant of the old civilization – let's call it an Atlantean civilization – and it is most likely a remnant of the former copper ore mine, which was formed at a time when on our continent, our ancestors dressed in animal skins and with flint axes, hunted mammoths.

We'll start with the location. This cave is most likely located on the Slovak-Polish border in the area limited by the Stara Lubovnia, Plavec roads, the Plavec-Muszyna railway line, the Muszyna-Żegiestów, Piwniczna road on the Polish side, and the Piwniczna-Stara, Lubovnia road. The Americans located the outlet of this cave and the crescent shaft near Sulín.

In the Middle Ages and later, until the end of the 18th century, iron, antimony, arsenic, silver, and copper ores were mined in northern Slovakia – what we know from city and parish chronicles and *spiski* of treasure hunters from the Brotherhood of the Seven Stars and other organizations, and individual seekers.

They were usually poor nest deposits, less often vain ones, with time fully exploited. Only holes in the ground and field names remained: Koperszady, Koprowa Dolina, Szpiglasowa Przełęcz, Miedziane Ławki, etc. - this was particularly evident in the German-language naming used at the time of the Austro-Hungarian Monarchy. I assume, therefore, that the crescent shaft was carved in limestone rock in the place where there was a nest of copper ore, the remains of which Dr. Antonin Horák took for the lining of unknown metal.

I reviewed the list of minerals that could play the role of this unknown metal and it turned out that several copper ores match the description, whose properties are given below:

Properties of some copper ores.

Mineral name	Chemical formula	Color
Native copper	Cu	Red, cover of the passivation layer of black
Tetrahedrit	$Cu_{12}Sb_4S_{13}$	steel-gray
Stannite	Cu_2FeSnS	gray, crystal
Covellite	CuS	blue-black
Bournonite	$PbCuSbS_3$	gray-black
Libethenite	$Cu_2(OH)PO_4$	green-black
Agardite	$(REE,CaH)Cu_6[(OH)_6(AsO_4) \cdot 3H_2O]$	Red, cover of the passivation layer of black

REE are radioactive rare earth elements (uranium, thorium, radium, polonium, cerium, etc.). Copper and its compounds dye the flame of the Bunsen burner a beautiful green color. This can explain the green and blue sparks struck from the walls with the impact of the bullets from the weapon of Capt. Horak. The presence of copper compounds can also explain the sharp smell of dust from the shaft walls. Copper compounds, especially sulphides and sulphates, easily react with water to release toxic hydrogen sulphide - H_2S or sulfur oxides - SO_x, which explains what Slavek said about poisonous gases deep in the cave... In addition, they have a characteristic, pungent and unpleasant smell, which is their hallmark.

Copper crystals are heavy and cannot be easily peeled off from the ground. It is also difficult to scratch them with a knife because they are hard but fragile. The presence of copper compounds in the crescent shaft explains all the phenomena observed by Dr. Horák.

Therefore, it would appear that the crescent shaft was a trace of some mining works carried out during the inhabitation of these areas by cave bears - *Ursus spealeus*, which became extinct in Europe after the last glacial, or 10-12 thousand years ago. At the same time, Platonic Atlantis fell.

There is a possibility given by Dr. Moore, who suggests that the Moon Shaft is a natural creation, formed as a result of leaching limestone from between two layers of the chert. The chert is organic or chemical hydrated silica - SiO2nH2O, which is deposited in thin layers in sedimentary rocks (e.g. in sandstones) or concretions (e.g. in carbonate rocks – limestone). Its layers are silky smooth with a greasy gloss and a hardness of 6.0^o on the Mochs scale, gray or brown and cryptocrystalline or amorphous.

The cherts are semi-precious stones: agates, chalcedonies, jaspers, onyxes, chrysoprases, carnelians, opals, and spinels. It should be noted here that onyx is black or black and blue. However, one fundamental objection arises: after all, Dr. Horák was a geologist, and he shouldn't have found it difficult to identify silica and its varieties, so this "explanation" doesn't add anything new to the case, but quite the opposite. (Cf.

"Encyklópedie Zeme," Bratislava 1986; Fuller S. - "Skały i minerały," Warsaw 1996; Hofmann H. - "Minerały," Warsaw 2001; Medenbach O., Sussieck-Fornfeld C. - "Minerały," Warsaw 1996; Bauer J. - "Skały i minerały," Warsaw 1997; "Minerały i kamienie szlachetne," Warsaw 1996; "Atlas mineralogii," Warsaw 2000.)

Let's hope that we can finally find it. This would be another evidence of the existence of an ancient, highly developed Atlantean civilization that disappeared in unexplained circumstances 120 centuries ago.

When we followed the mysterious journal of Capt. Horák, in which he described his adventures in a mysterious cave, we hoped that we would be able to learn more about the people who were associated with this story. Over time, it turned out that this was not as easy as it might seem, but after a closer look at the whole story and checking several data related to the characters presented in the event diary, some conclusions come to mind. Let's start with recapitulating our knowledge about these people or groups of people who are *dramatis personae*:

* Battalion: Until October 20, 1944, he took part in two battles, during which the entire unit of commissariat fell into the hands of the enemy. The enemy destroyed the entire food supply system and the soldiers had nothing to eat, except cornbread, which was very little.

The number of soldiers and officers on October 21, 1944, was 184 people, of whom 25% were wounded and 16 on stretchers. It follows that this unit only had ⅓ of its original state, i.e. about 200 soldiers. On October 21, the remains of the battalion were retreating along the northern slope of the mountains, probably to the east. At dawn on October 22, they were attacked by a Wehrmacht unit and shot at with two 70 mm guns from a distance of about 300 meters. The battle lasted about 12 hours. From October 23, the battalion was retreating towards Košice, and around October 27, 1944, it was dislocated east of Košice, where it was waiting for the Red Army to join it.

* Company: (belonged to the above-mentioned battalion). Around October 20, its commander was Capt. Dr. Antonin T. Horák, and its private soldiers, Private Jurek and Martin (the latter died on October 27, 1944). During the retreat of the battalion on October 20-22, 1944, the company was in the rearguard and for 12 hours was protecting the retreat of the main forces. Then Capt. Horak ordered detachment from the enemy. When retreating, two grenades fell into the left trench and two soldiers were wounded. The company commander who went there was attacked by the enemy and received several wounds from a bayonet, shot at his left hand and a blow to the head, after which, he lost consciousness. All the wounded were left on the battlefield and the rest of the company managed to retreat. The local host hid them from the Germans.

* Capt. Dr. Antonin T. Horák: (company commander). He had an academic education. In the fight against the Wehrmacht on October 22, 1944, he was wounded in the left arm and in the head. He was unconscious on the battlefield. The local host hid him for several days. He joined the company around November 5, 1944, near Koš ice.

* Martin: (company soldier), he was wounded in the stomach during the clash with Wehrmacht on October 22, 1944. The wound was very deep. He stayed on the battlefield and hid with Capt. Dr. Horák. He died on the night of October 26/27, 1944. He was buried in the trench in which he was wounded. I hoped to, if not solve it completely, then at least approach the final solution of the shaft puzzle. Over time, it turned out that this was not as easy as it might seem, but after a closer look at the whole story and checking several data related to the characters presented in the event diary, some conclusions came to mind. In the spring of 1945, his host put a cross on grace. His death certificate was issued by Capt. Dr. Antonin T. Horák. Jurek, a company soldier,

who lived in Bratislava and was a carpenter by profession. In October 1944 he was either a bachelor or divorced. His father was in the USA before the war. He knew Martin and his family. In the battle with the Wehrmacht, he was wounded by a grenade shard in his thigh. He stayed on the battlefield and then hid with Dr. Horák, with whom he joined the company near Košice on November 5. After the war, he married Hanka, the daughter of shepherd Slavek.

* Place of battle and being wounded: slopes of the Tatras, northern slope with trenches. Martin was buried in one of them, and a cross was to be placed on his grave. The surrounding pastures belonged to Slavek.

* Slavek: shepherd, owner of several pastures, host. He belonged to the old settlers in these parts as his father and grandfather lived there. He had two daughters – Hanka and Olga.

* Hanka: in October 1944 she was nubile. After the war, she probably married a private Jurek, a carpenter from Bratislava. Capt. Horak gave her a letter to a jeweler friend to give her a druse of Czech garnets as a wedding present.

* Location of the Moon Cave (according to data from 1944): not overgrown, steep slope (there were avalanches). The road from the battlefield to the cave took Slavek and one slightly wounded man, who were carrying two seriously wounded people, up to 4 hours. Mountain pine was on the route between the battlefield and the cave.

* Description of the cave: a narrow passage led to the spacious room. Next was a narrow passage to a maze full of chasms and sources emitting poisonous gases (SO_2, SO, H_2S, CH_4, CO, CO_2), but there were bats in the cave. This would indicate that there couldn't be toxic CO or CH_4 gases in the cave, because bats couldn't live in a poisoned atmosphere.

As the first Moon Cave interested the "secret hunters" known in the Czech Republic as, engineer Ivan Mackerle and Michał Brumlik, who made their first trip to Slovakia on October 7-11,

1982. The purpose of the expedition was to verify some basic data, such as:

1. Determining the location of the Moon Cave on the map according to the information contained in the work of Jacques Bergier;
2. Finding people who knew the place of entry into the Moon Cave, i.e. Capt. Dr. A. T. Horák, Jurek, Slavek, his daughter and their relatives;
3. Checking and making comparisons with the Capt. Horák's records, descriptions of fights between the SNU insurgent units and the Wehrmacht forces and those subordinate to pr. Tiso;
4. Finding landmarks listed in the journal of Capt. Horák, which could help in locating the Moon Cave.

("Zpráva o pátraní po tajemn šachté ve tvaru pulměsíce dle údaju from the knihy of Jacqu Bergier" Le livre de l´ inexplicable ", AIM, Cesta from 7-11 Oct. 1982" (typescript), Prague 10.17.1982, p. 1-9)

This expedition brought tangible results – the section where the Moon Cave was to be located was to be on the Levoča Hills, which since 1952 have been a military training ground. You can enter there only after presenting a special pass. Its geographical location was also specified: 49°02'N - 020° 07'E with an accuracy of 10', which corresponds to the coordinates: 49° 12'N - 020° 17'E, the next location indicates the place located in the Levoča Mountains, on position 49° 12'N - 020° 44'E). As for the location in the Levoča Mountains area, the cave should be located south of the village of Jakubany, between the Kečera and Magurič mountains. The investigation carried out in the villages of Jakubany, Kolačkov, Šambron and Bajerovce, brought another fact. Well, during World War II, there was no host in these places who had only two daughters with such names. In October 1944, there were no fights, and there were no insurgent troops in the strength of a battalion or even a company. There were no guerrilla groups at all.

A retired colonel told the researchers that he wasn't aware of any guerrilla unit that fought the Wehrmacht, east of Levoča on October 22, 1944. This was the most critical phase of the SNU, when insurgent forces were pushed towards the High Tatras, where they changed from a regular to a guerrilla fight. It is unlikely that someone was heading east, but this possibility cannot be totally excluded. For example, it could have been a group of soldiers who decided to reach their homes. To this end, they selected a commander from among them, which is why their march was organized in a military fashion.

During the investigation, people were asked about the word "Yzdar," which was supposed to be the name of the place where shepherd Slavek was to stay temporarily after the war. In two independent cases, appeared the name of the place Ždiar, where, indeed, they were shepherds, and the surname Slavek could appear there. Unfortunately, even the oldest residents in Ždiar claimed that no shepherd Slavek or any fights between Slovak patriots and Wehrmacht took place in October or other months of 1944.

The Second expedition of Eng. Mackerly and Brumlik took place on July 12-21, 1984 and its purpose was to identify the place of the skirmish of Capt. Horák with Germans, examine the nationality and identity of the people appearing in this event and find their relatives. (See "Zpráva o pátraní po Měsíční šachtě dle údaju amerického speleologického časopisu NSS News č.3 3/1965, Aim, Cesta from July 12-21, 1984," Prague 1984, p. 1-6)

The Capt. Horák's journal shows that Slavek's family belonged to old settlers, indigenous peoples. Slavek claimed that he visited the cave with his father and grandfather, so it is highly probable that his daughters were also born there. In 1944, partisan Jurek wanted to marry Hanka, so she could be 15-20 years old at that time, which would mean that she was born between 1916 and 1929. If Olga was younger, then she would be under 8 years old, and thus, she couldn't go with her father to the mountains. Therefore, all girls named Hanka (Hana or in Polish Hanna, Anna) and Oľga (Olga), born between 1916 and 1936 were sought. The name Hanka or Hana is a Czech name and isn't often used in Slovakia, but as in Poland, Anna is called Hanna. In the metrical lists from January 1, 1923, to December 31, 1949, there were only two Olga and a few Annas, with NO Anna WITH THE SAME SURNAME matching ANY Olga, and none of them had a father named Slavek or Slav (Slavomir). What's more, the name Hana is not there at all.

The metrical records from the period from January 1, 1907, to December 31, 1922, also doesn't contain the names Olga and Hana – there are only three Annas, but NONE of them had "Slav" in their surname. The above findings cannot, however, constitute the final argument as all the listed persons could use their middle names, as is practiced, for example, in Lesser Poland, or nicknames that in the case of Slavek the shepherd. After all, there was a war. Thus, first or last name Slavek could have been a guerrilla nickname and this man could be called completely different and not be who he claimed to be. He may have been an employee of some Allied intelligence, hence the secret surrounding him.

Similarly, the search in Liptovská Osada and Liptovská Nižna brought negative results – in 1916-1929 no men with the surname Slav or similar had newborn daughters Olga and Hana.

A former colonel from the 6th Tactical Group "Zobor," which operated in the areas where Capt. Horák's sub-unit was located, stated that he knew nothing about the existence of an officer with that name and added some more information:

1. NO battalion or other sub-unit was retreating towards Košice. All units went towards the Tatra Mountains,

where they were disbanded. Soldiers who belonged to them either returned to their homes or fought in partisan groups - also in Poland, until 1945;

2. Until October 28, 1944, there was no snow in this area... Only on October 28, it began to snow. A lot of snow fell only after November 3, 1944.

Therefore, this analysis didn't lead to any specific conclusions. Not one person who knew the location of the Moon Cave could be identified:

- Capt. Horák was not known by the local inhabitants or soldiers of the insurgent army;
- shepherd Slavek with his two daughters Olga and Hanka never lived in the northern part of the Levoča Mountains, as well as in the town of Ždiar (Yzdar). In the Levoča Mountains area, the surname Slavek doesn't occur.

Also, the information contained in the journal of Cpt. Horák couldn't be confirmed:

- October 22, 1944, no skirmish occurred in this area;
- Neither the inhabitants nor the foresters knew anything about the grave of the insurgent in this area;
- There are no pines or mugo pines in the Levoča Mountains area;
- There is no information about snowfall at the end of October 1944, (Ibid, p. 9)

Further investigation brought another result - the coordinates of the place where the Moon Cave was to be located, given by NSS News were trumped up by the editor-in-chief of "NSS News," Dr. G. Moore, who gave them according to the abbreviated version of Dr. Horák's diary and not very accurate map of Czechoslovakia. This version was given by Thomas de Jean in "Księga Tajemnic 2."

It was assumed *a priori* that the Moon Cave is located on the northern slope of the Low Tatras, which corresponded to Dr. Horák's assertion that the cave is located on the northern side of the Tatra Mountains; that at the end of the war, shepherd Slavek lived temporarily in Ždiar, about fights with Germans, about the occurrence of mugo pines, and so on, and so forth. Selection of the place near Liptovská Osada, between L'ubochňou and Parnicou (Thomas de Jean gives the place names as "Plavince" and "Lubocna") as we already know, didn't work out. It didn't match the facts.

One thing that has been proven with one hundred percent certainty is that all dates placing these events at the time are FALSE. For example, a strong snowfall occurred on November 3, 1944, and there was no snow on October 22, which is in direct contradiction to what Dr. Horák writes. The conclusion follows, which seems to confirm the obvious fact that Dr. Horák wrote his diary not on the spot, but much later. – namely in 1965, when he didn't remember the events accurately. The battle with the Nazis took place not on October 22, but on November 3, 1944. Therefore, you can't use Dr. Horák's records to determine historical events. (AIM, private correspondence from February 19, 1991)

A further premise for the location of the Moon Cave would be the presence of limestone in Slovakia. The described underground spaces were supposed to be in limestone rocks. To this end, basic reference points and limestone rock areas should be mapped. They would have to be accurate enough to locate a small limestone nest in a different rock around it (in the case of the Moon Cave, in sandstone), and such structures exist in northern Slovakia. These are the Belianske Tatras.

The explanation given by the geologist from Ústřední ústav geologický in Prague is also interesting because he believes what

Dr. Horák wrote about the cave and his achievements, although it is a subjective view. For example, it seems strange that in the journal, he doesn't mention a word about the sizes that characterize the underground world of caves. This would prove that Capt. Horák was interested not so much in the details of the penetrated surroundings, as in his own interests and insights. In other words, he relied more on his own feelings than on a reasonably objective description of the exact circumstances that accompanied the events of many years ago. This confirms that the journal was written a little later as "memories of better times." For example, the descriptive phrase: *in the Tatra Mountains* may or may not mean the Tatra Mountains as such, but other mountain ranges located nearby. Another information: *at Zdar* indicates that it may be the town of Ždiar in the area of the Belianske Tatras. (See "Zpráva o jednání," AIM, Ústřední ústav geologický, Prague Oct. 7, 1988, p. 2)

Further searches brought slightly more information about the identity of Capt. Dr. Antonin T. Horák. According to the currently obtained information, he was an officer in the rank of captain, who was probably thrown into the territory of Slovakia, in the airborne brigade composed of Czechs and Slovaks in the USSR, who had previously fought in the British RAF. After the war, he left Czechoslovakia and moved to the USA, where from 1965, he lived in Pueblo (Colorado). He was a doctor of linguistics and a restaurant owner. His wife's name was Anna. He died in June 1976. No trace of his relatives or friends was found in Czechoslovakia. In the editorial office of the magazine published by the U.S.S. Geological Survey, this author was no longer remembered. The editor Dr. G. Moore wrote back to Mackerly, that information about the latitude and longitude of the Moon Cave, he thought up himself, looking at the map of Czechoslovakia, and they didn't need to be specific. (Letter of George W. Moor to engineer Mackerly of March 27, 1983) How he came to the names "Plavnica" and "Lubocna," he didn't know, and in the original text of Dr. Horák, there is nothing about them. It is quite likely that Dr. Horák mentioned them when meeting Dr. Moore, but it is not known in what context.

The first trip, which took place on October 7-11, 1982, was guided by the given coordinates of longitude and latitude. The researchers also assumed that there was a printing mistake: Lubocna = Lubovňa, etc. because in the place with the given coordinates there are two towns - Stara Lubovňa and Plavnica. The expedition has set such goals:

1. Find the place of skirmishes according to the journal's instructions;
2. Determine the fate and get more information about Dr. Horák's subunit. It is known that he had 184 soldiers marching towards Košice, which was unusual in itself because the vast majority of the SNU insurgents were heading towards Banská Bystrica, or their troops were disbanded, and they went home;
3. Get more details about Cpt. Dr. Horák, date and place of his birth, which would allow us to reconstruct his biography and battle route;
4. Find more information about Jurek, who knows where the cave is but does not know its secret. He married Slavek's daughter and then was a carpenter in Bratislava;
5. Find Slavek the shepherd in Ždiar.

Since the snow fell after November 1, 1944, it is known that the dates of the battles were invented. Dr. Horák probably didn't write any journal at all and wrote his memories in the form of a diary to make them more attractive to the publisher. He didn't remember the exact dates, so he just came up with them. The fact that it was deep snow, he couldn't forget it, he didn't invent it - so it was in November when the Slovak National Uprising was over and the insurgent army was disbanded. So, it could only be a group of insurgents returning home, without any military organization.

The military unit, this battalion, couldn't be identified either through the archives of the SNU Museum in Banská Bystrica, at the *Matica Slovenska* in Martin, Oddeleni Vojenské Dejiny Slovenska in Bratislava, or interviews with soldiers and officers of the Slovak Army.

As for Ždiar, apart from the village at the foot of the Belianske Tatras, there are: Ždiar at Liptovska Tepličke, Ždiar near Rožnava, Ždiar at Nižnom Slavkove, and Ždiar at Svidnik. As for the name "Lubocna," it was hypothesized that it could be L'ubochňa and Parnica (instead of Plavnica), where Ždiar is also nearby. Maybe it is a typographical error when writing Slovak names but the possibilities of verifying this hypothesis are practically zero.

It is a pity that the whole story seems to be stalled and at the moment there is little probability of its final resolution. Let's hope that Dr. Miloš Jesenský will not give up so easily and we will hear about it someday, although the tangle of names and locations confuses the whole matter, which in 99.999999% seems to be only a paleocontact hoax - a stupid joke made for. Exactly, is it only for fame and money? It just doesn't seem so certain. It is hard to believe that for a few dollars and a few days of glory, Dr. Horák released such nonsense into print. This is not what people who have gone through the hell of war and uprising do. It doesn't suit these types of people.

It seems to me that the most likely location is the one from the Belianske Tatras, which I show on map II. At the point marked with the number "9" is the intersection of geographical coordinates - 49° 12 'N - 020° 17' E, i.e. on the slopes of Stežky, which is part of the granite massif of the High Tatras, and there are no caves in this area. If we look a little further north, then on the North slope of the Belianske Tatras we will find Babia Dolina, wherein the coordinates 49 ° 15 'N - 020 ° 17' E could be the sough-after cave. Of course, this is only a guess, but almost all location conditions given by Dr. Horák are met. It is a pity that there, as in the case of Levoča Mountains, is a military training ground, and over the rest of the Belian Tatras the veil of secrecy is spread by TANAP.

The strange fact is that only three tourist routes run through the Belianske Tatras: blue-green trail No. 2911/5810 on the southern side of the Belianske Tatras, yellow No. 8862 to Belianska Cave and green No. 5811 to Magura and Rigelsky Potok. From 1995, there is available the so-called "Scientific path" from Rigelsky Potok to the wide mountain pass to trail 2911/5810. Who wants tourists not to wander around the Belianske Tatras? TANAP? Perhaps, because trees are being cut there and thousands of cubic meters of wood are being exported per year, and the strict nature reserve that is there, is in name only. ("Tygodnik Podhalański" No. 49.50,51/1995)

Around the Belianske Tatras, there are several holiday houses of Prague - now Bratislava - VIPs, which before 1990 were protected by elite units of the Ministry of the Interior. Is that all the well-trained Št. B. commandos protected? Or maybe something more, such as the Moon Cave? It is to be hoped that the cave was not "looted," and its secrets transported to the basements of Łubianka or Chodynka, where secrets originating from Warsaw Pact countries usually found their way. I will only mention Polish Gdynia incident of 1959, when a humanoid was found on the Gdynia beach, transported under escort to the USSR (Apparently, however, this EBE is in Poland, well hidden in the morgue of the university hospital in Gdynia - sic.). This could be the case with the Moon Cave, V-7, Nazi A bomb and many, many other secrets. I don't think that the secret of the Moon Cave will come to light in this millennium, simply because such outsiders like Dr. Jesenský are doing the research. As long as there is a conspiracy of silence in which, along with decision-makers, the flower of our science also takes part, this and other riddles will remain a part of the "Great Unknown."

There is a Polish accent throughout this history. There is something disturbingly familiar in Dr. Horák's notes, I would say, homely, which I have read somewhere before. Indeed, we remembered the material about the existence of "Glassy tunnels" in the Slovakian slope of Babia Góra. These stories are so similar that there can be no accidental coincidence. It seems to me that the convergence of these two legends is not entirely accidental, and there's more to it than just blind chance. Was the mysterious informant of Dr. Jan Pająk telling him his version of the Legend of the Moon Cave, only slightly modifying and adapting it to the reality of the Beskids? It seems that this was the case, but it wasn't about the slopes of Babia Góra, but about the slopes of Babia Dolina in the Belianske Tatras. (Jesenský M. : Tajemnica Księżycowej Jaskini, "Wizje Peryferyjne", No. 2/1996, p. 22-29)

CHAPTER 3

The Riddle of the Glassy Tunnels

We get acquainted with Dr. Jan Pająk - An unusual story from Wincenty's childhood - A well-guarded highlander's secret: Tunnels under Babia Góra? - Further comments and observations.

In the previous chapter, we expressed an attractive hypothesis that the Moon Cave and the system of glassy tunnels under Babia Góra, about which writes the Polish scientist, Dr. Eng. Jan Pająk, are two aspects of the same problem. In accordance with the principle of *audiatur altra pars*, we first pass extensive fragments of the accounts of prof. Pająk (Leśniakiewicz R. : "Księżycowa Jaskinia - zagadki ciąg dalszy," "Wizje peryferyjne," No. 3/1996, p. 24-28):

"I was in high school graduating class when I heard the first tale of glassy tunnels that looked like they had been melted in a rock by a huge machine. The person who told me about them, let's call him Vincenty, was known to me from other unusual stories that collided drastically with my "scientific worldview." When I listened to this story, I didn't pay special attention to it and treated it as entertainment. Over time, I forgot some details, for example, I'm not sure if the tunnel started on Babia or Barania Góra, where it led, how it was marked, how to open it, and so on, and so forth. Hence, I quote a loose story, which I remember now.

As usual with the winters of the 1960s, the power plant turned off the power again that evening. So, we sat by the buzzing stove listening to the crackling of flames. After a while, Vincenty began: "When I was your age, one evening my father announced that the next morning we would go a long way. In the morning I was surprised that instead of the usual preparations for the fair, my father packed only an oil lantern, matches, and a supply of food. My curiosity grew even more when we set out on foot, instead of a wagon, as usual. When we left the village, the guiding father called me in silence.

"Vicek," he said, "it's time for you to learn the secret of our ancestors. This secret has been passed down from father to son since old times. We keep it in the family for a rainy day. Apart from me, a few family members scattered over other villages know about it. This secret is a hidden underground passage. Watch the road now, because I will show you it only once. You have to remember it well."

We continued our journey in silence. We approached the foothills of Babia Góra from the Czech side (the author probably meant the Slovak side because neither Babia nor Barania Góra has slopes on the Czech side of the border. Both of these mountains lie a little further east of the Slovak-Czech [ethnic and administrative] border. - note RKL) - *my father stopped again and showed me a rock at a height of about 1/3 of this mountain.*

"Vicek," he said, "note this rock because it covers the entrance to the underground."

When we climbed the rock, I was surprised that no passage could be seen. My father leaned his back at the corner and started pushing. I stood surprised because up close, the rock looked too big for one man to push.

"Damn," father swore, "not opened for long, it had to jam up. Don't stare. Help me push." I jumped and pushed, the rock budged and after the initial resistance, moved surprisingly lightly. An entrance large enough to go through on the cart got revealed. My

father lit a kerosene lantern, then pushed the rock to the previous place. It covered the entrance opening completely. Then he began to walk down the tunnel that started from this rock and led quite steeply down. I was stunned because I haven't seen anything like this in my life. The tunnel was huge and in it would fit not only the car but even the whole train. It ran straight like an arrow. Its cross-section was circular, but a little flattened from above. The surface was slightly wavy as if notched with the edge of a huge drill. The walls were glistening as if covered by glass. Although it came down abruptly, it was amazingly dry, with no sign of water flowing down the floor and walls. I also noticed that our shoes walking on the glassy floor didn't emit any sound that would be expected on a rock, the sound of footsteps was muffled as if the floor of the tunnel had been lined with some material.

After quite a long march, the tunnel fell into a huge barrel-shaped chamber standing slightly obliquely. The walls of this chamber were glassy, like the walls of the tunnel we came in, but they were not notched, and the floor and walls were formed in some strange spiral pattern, looking like a frozen vortex. The outlets of several tunnels converged in this chamber. Some of them were round, some triangular. My father laid the lantern on the ground and sat down for a moment to rest, and I began to look around the cavern. Under the walls, away from the tunnel outlets, the floor was littered with objects, chests, barrels and various weapons. I saw parts of knight's armor, clubs, swords, sabers, as well as antique firearms. My attention was drawn to an unusual, beautiful shotgun with a richly inlaid white-butt barrel.

I took this shotgun to look at it, but my father shouted at me, "Don't move. We don't have any oil to grease it again."

"We can take it," I replied.

"No," my father said, "all this have to wait here in case of hard times." I sat down with my father. Then he began to explain, "The tunnels you see here lead to every country and every continent. So, you can get through them wherever you like; of course, if you know

how to move in them. This tunnel on the left leads to Germany, then to England, then to America, where it connects to the tunnel on the right. The tunnel on the right leads to Russia, then to the Caucasus and China, then to Japan and finally to America. You can also reach America by remaining tunnels leading under the Earth's poles. Each of these tunnels has from time to time a branching chamber similar to the one in which we are now, where it connects with other tunnels going in different directions. It's easy to get lost in this maze. That's why our ancestors used signs that informed which tunnel to choose. Come on, I'll show you what these signs look like."

We went into one of the tunnels and then at its outlet, I noticed dozens of clumsy drawings scribbled with black paint or dried blood. My father showed me drawing by drawing, explaining its meaning. One of them meant Wawel in Cracow [.].

When he was explaining the signs to me, unexpectedly there was a sound of rumbling, hissing and metallic screeching – it was like a passing steam train when it switches rails on the points or brakes.

Father fell silent and said, "I will explain the rest on the way back, now we must return quickly." We began to climb quickly through the entrance shaft, chased by an ever louder rumble and metallic squeal. My father was clearly worried and often looked back. When we reached the rocks at the entrance, the hiss and squeak were as loud as if the train had braked just behind us. After stepping outside and moving the rock, my father breathless, fell to the ground.

After a long rest, he began to explain, "The tunnels you saw were not made by humans, but by all-powerful creatures that live underground. These creatures use tunnels to move underground from one side of the world to the other. They use fiery flying machines for this purpose. If such a machine ran us down, we would be inevitably baked from its heat. Fortunately, the voice in the tunnel carries a long way, so it's time to get out of its way when you hear it. In addition, these creatures live in other parts of the world and come here very rarely. Our ancestors used these tunnels to hide from invaders and quickly march in other directions." On the way back, my father explained to me the meaning of the other signs. He also told me to pass this knowledge to someone else in good time so that it would not be forgotten. (Pająk J., Pańszczyk K. - "Tunele NOL spod Babiej Góry", Nowy Targ - Kota Samarahan 1998 [script].)

This ends the account of the man named Vincenty, the informer of Dr. Jan Pająk, who in turn quoted these stories as proof of the existence of magnocraft –flying machines similar in appearance to Unidentified Flying Objects or UFOs – and in fact, probably having identical propulsion.

The origin of this tunnel is also another matter - probably a remnant of beings inhabiting the interior of our planet after something like Agarta or Shangri-la. The famous esoterics and exotericists wrote about it: **M. Bławatska and Ferdynand Antoni Ossendowski, Brinsley le Poer-Trench and Mircea Eliade, Aleksander Grobicki, and Umberto Eco.** (See also Ossendowski AF - "Przez kraj ludzi, zwierząt i bogów," Poznań 1930; Grobicki Al. - "Nie tylko Trójkąt Bermudzki," Gdańsk 1980; Krzystak J., "Däniken, Kosmici i Atlantydzi =," Katowice 1997; Maclellean A .- "Zaginiony świat Agharti", Warsaw 1996; Maclellan A. - "Tajemnica Pustej Ziemi," Warsaw 2000; Zajdler L. - "Atlantis," Warsaw 1980.) But more on that later. Now, let's deal with the common points of both legendary singularities of the Moon Cave and glassy tunnel.

These points have already been highlighted in the text of the report of prof. Pająk, but I will remind you of them again:

- The location of both caves (because the tunnel in question will still be called "the cave") is a secret kept in families for many (at least several) generations.

- This secret is passed from father to son. Slavek didn't have a son, so most likely he didn't pass on the secret, or passed it to one of the descendants in the family of his brothers or sisters.
- The secret would be a hidden underground or an underground passage lying in areas belonging to one family, quite prosperous – as it results from the account.
- Description of the cave: huge sizes, slightly undulating walls and flooring, smooth walls lined with some unusual material (in the account of Prof. Pająk) or metal. There is no water flowing down the walls, although there is a talk about stalactites and stalagmites, but they are outside, the right cave. Its shape is very unusual – an inclined barrel or an inclined shaft with a crescent shape. The triangular shape of the corridors also makes both legends similar.

Phenomena occurring in caves. It is about acoustic phenomena, the source of which is human or Alien Being activities. In both cases, it comes down to rumbling and metallic hissing or screeching.

- Both caves are located in Slovakia. Of course, there are some differences in both accounts, but the conclusion is the same.
- Both caves were built by unknown constructors, who are identified with ancient "Platonic" or extraterrestrial civilizations.

Where is the entrance to the glassy tunnel? Vincenty's report speaks about the Slovak side of Babia Góra. Barania Góra is out of the question, and this is because its southern slopes were not crossed by the state border, which runs through Babia Góra. In light of Vincenty's account, the entrance is located at ⅔ of the relative height of the mountain, i.e. about 1,200 m a.s.l., in the Bystra stream valley. The problem is that apart from the summit of Diablak, which is a rocky "island" in the surrounding area, on the southern slopes of Babia Góra there are no rocks. This is a certainty and the first objection.

The second objection concerns the contradiction in Vincenty's account since the corridor markings were made with poor paint or blood; how did they survive the terrible (apparently) heat of the underground aircraft moving through corridors and chambers? How did the wooden or canvas items of everyday use gathered there last this heat? After all, they should have been destroyed at the first passage of the "underground" UFO, right? So, the heat emitted by these vehicles was not as terrible as Vincenty said. Or, maybe it was ionizing radiation? Radial burns give a picture similar to conventional thermal burns, so maybe this was what Vincenty meant? Interesting, because Dr. Horák also assumed that the Moon Cave is an excavation after uranium ore mining, as suggested by Thomas de Jean.

That's why we suspect that the tunnel is de facto the Moon Cave, and Vincenty, claiming that the corridor outlet is in Babia Góra, simply led prof. Pająk to a dead end. Why would he have told him the truth anyway? Since the existence of the corridor is such a secret, why only for prof. Pająk would he have broken the silence? After all, information about the caves was kept secret and breaking the secret would be tantamount to breaking the law of *omertà*. For this simple reason, the account of Vincenty and then of prof. Pająk in this regard is not reliable. Again, there is the supposition that this is about Babia Dolina in the Belian Tatras. It's difficult to assume that there were two different formations with such unusual properties.

Therefore, one more observation arises – Vincenty talks about family members who know the secret of the inhabitants of other villages. Well, many families have relatives in Slovakia and vice-versa, so in Poland and Slovakia, the legend should be known to many people. Professor Pająk doesn't write where he met with Vincenty, but I bet it took place either in Zakopane or in Podhale, and not in Zawoja or in Polish or Slovak Orava. So, it seems that Vincenty and Dr. Horák have come across the same secret.

CHAPTER 4

Treasure Hunters versus the Spanish *Securitate*

An exotic legend or truth - Sebastian Berzeviczy enters the stage - Testimony of Pastor Bucholtz - Who was the Spanish *Securitate* looking for?

The idea of combining these two Legends came to our minds when in the mid-90s we were collecting materials for our first joint book on the space technologies of Nazi Germany. Already then, we had another hypothesis that the Moon Cave could be located in the Pieniny, where the local tradition combines the legends of the Inca treasures with the nobleman, traveler, and adventurer **Sebastian Berzeviczy**. When we thoroughly analyzed this story, we thought that in our book there should be a place for this condottiere – his extraordinary adventures in the New World, exotic and great love, betrayal and death, royal envoys and, of course, huge treasures hidden in caves (Jesenský M. : "Posledný Inkov odkaz I. – III," "Slovenské národné noviny," vol. 12 (16), No. 12 (5.6.2001), p. 9, No. 13 (19.6.2001), p. 9, no. 14 (3.7.2001), p. 9, Leśniakiewicz R. : "Księżycowa jaskinia na Spiszu?", "Świat UFO," vol. 22, No. 1 (67) (2002), p. 89 -99).

In 1946, in the Dunajec Castle in Niedzica, on the Polish-Slovak border river Dunajec, a certain **Andrzej Benesz** appeared with a will, which his father received from the Cracovian church of the Holy Cross. This document was written at the end of the 18th century in the Dunajec castle by Sebastian Berzevicz and the envoys who came to the castle from Peru. Benesz, accompanied by a local village head, commander of the Citizens' Militia station and officer of the Border Protection Forces, broke the last step of the stairs leading to the castle and there he found a metal tube containing a document in the form of an Indian quipu. It consisted of three strings looped in numerous knots and ending with unusual plaques with Latin inscriptions: "Titicaca," "Vigo," and "Dunajec." The Indian quipu was to be a clue to the location of a huge Indian treasure, whose heir was to be the grandson of Berzeviczy - **Antonio Berzeviczy aka Benesz alias Condorcanqui aka Tupac Amaru III**. So far, there is no expert who would solve this mystery of a nobleman who ruled the Niedzica castle for so many years.

Sebastian, driven by the desire to gain fame, fortune, and adventure, got to the court of the Spanish king, from where he was sent to Peru, where he faithfully served the Spanish crown. There he married an Indian princess, in which veins flowed the royal blood of the Incas. From this marriage, their daughter **Umina** was born, who married the last pretender to the Inca throne – **Jose Gabriel** or **Gabriel Condorcanqui aka Tupac Amaru II**, who in the years 1779-81 led the uprising against the Spaniards. After the cruel suppression of the rebellion and the murder of Tupac Amaru II, Sebastian managed to escape with Umina and Antonio to the Old World, but the vengeful hand of the Spanish crown reached the refugees in Venice. Another escape to the Dunajec was not a detachment from the persecutors. Umin was murdered in the castle, where her ghost apparently frightens to this day.

Berzeviczy understood that his grandson was not safe there and secretly sent him to the Moravian Krumlov, where he prepared a false identity for him in the Benesz family. Antonio, now Antonin Benesz, took the name of his foster parents. The Benesz family became Polonized thanks to marriages and led a meager life on the northern side of the Carpathians (See:

Rowiński A. : "Pod klątwą kapłanów," Warsaw, 2000; Leśniakiewicz W. - "Skarb Inków - Szukajcie, ale czy znajdziecie?" w "Odkrywca" No. 6/2002).

Here our search for answers begins. Berzeviczy, of all people, wasn't stupid. Sebastian Berzeviczy, if he were to hide his treasures somewhere, then only in the mountains, and more precisely in the caves. Niedzica or Tropsztyn Castle could be penetrated by the "Spanish KGB" relatively easily, which was proved by the murder of Umina. But look for treasures in the Pieniny or Tatra caves – that's another matter. At that time these mountains were still relatively unknown and were penetrated only by highlanders and treasure hunters associated in the **Brotherhood of St. Laurence** also called the **Brotherhood of Seven Stars**, whose headquarters were located in Polish lands in two cities: Cracow, on the Small Market Square and Wroclaw, on the Salt Market. It was a supranational fraternity consisting of alchemists, globetrotters, loungers, ex-soldiers, townsfolk, and nobles – in a word, people of all social classes and nationalities, including the Spaniards, remaining at the service of the Inquisition and royal secret services.

Who knows if the said Brotherhood is not responsible for the mysterious death of one of the strangest people of the nineteenth century, living in Poland, having a German father and Polish after mother, widely-read writer, doctor, traveler, and adventurer – **Dr. Teodor Teudolta Tripplin**. If reincarnation exists, then its next incarnation was another restless spirit of Polish literature, this time one of the 20th century – **Antoni Ferdynand Ossendowski**. Both were dealing with treasures, both died in circumstances not explained to this day, and both were extremely popular in the country. Dr. Tripplin went to Italy, then to Spain, and after returning to the country, he immediately went to the Dunajec Castle and visited Spiš. He was nosy, very nosy. Mr. Rowiński is surprised that in all available work of Dr. Tripplin, there is not a word about the Incas, and will not be. Tripplin was just looking for facts and documents, and if I'm right, he was murdered in 1881 by someone who really didn't want them to see the light of day. Dr. Tripplin's documents and notes were destroyed or hidden so that no one would find them quickly. There is no place here for the Inca curse, but for a simple criminal case, in which curiosity about the world and the desire to investigate historical truth are intertwined with the desire for profit and revenge. Interested people should read the books of the Wroclaw historian **Dr. Jacek Kolbuszewski** – "Skarby Króla Gregoriusa," "Bractwo Siedmiu Gwiazd," "Dziwne podróże, dziwni podróżnicy," and more. "Bractwo Siedmiu Gwiazd" was the perfect cover for Spanish political intelligence, which allowed to eliminate Umina. The Niedzica hideout ceased to be safe and it was necessary to hide Antonio Benesz alias Berzeviczy aka Condorcanqui alias Tupac Amaru III in a different way – by adopting and blurring the lead. We only feel sorry for historians without a shred of imagination, who demanded documents and testimonies of witnesses. If Berzeviczy was counting on something, it was the kind of stupidity that mandates formalism in the search for a goal – Antonio was the goal in this case. Special services are guided by specific operational logic, which is based on information and prediction. Its opposite is a formal and rigid approach to the problem, the Spaniards made this mistake and Antonio survived (See: Kolbuszewski J. - "Dziwne podróże, dziwni podróżnicy," Katowice 1972).

The treasure was not found either, but I suspect that Umina had only a fraction of a percent of what the Inca managed to take away from Eldorado. If the treasure existed and was in Niedzica in the Dunajec Castle, it could have been sent to the place of deposit in three locations:

- Tropsztyn Castle by Czchów Lake and further to Gdansk, from where they were dispatched to Canada or Iceland or anywhere;

- Moon Cave in the Levoča Mountains or the Spiš Magura, or
- The Belianske Tatras or the High Tatras.

In the first case, the treasures flowed God only knows where. They could be in Iceland, northern Canada, and the bottom of the Atlantic. They may also be under the Tropsztyn Castle, but this is the least certain. In the second case, the most probable, Sebastian Berzeviczy and his Indians hid the treasure in some unknown cave, perhaps in the Moon Cave, which is supported by the facts described by pastor Buchholtz senior.

The third possibility is less likely because Sebastian Berzeviczy **knew** that the Belian, High, Low and Western Tatras are the subject of special exploration by the Brotherhood of the Seven Stars and agents of the "Spanish Securitate" camouflaging under this banner, who were just waiting for someone hid some valuables in the Tatras. Meanwhile, according to the records of Pastor Buchholtz, the Pieniny were already **depleted and explored** – after all, he writes about the old tunnels of copper mines. Therefore, hardly anyone would venture into these areas in search of anything. However, in her article, Wiktoria Leśniakiewicz claims that this magical Inca treasure de facto no longer exists. It was completely used up for the uprising of the Spring of Nations in Poland and Hungary, and besides, Berzeviczy had to provide the descendant of the Inca ruler with some decent living, didn't he? It's no use in looking for it and only a beautiful legend of five nations is left of it, unlike the Moon Cave, whose existence is a real fact (Leśniakiewicz W. - "Skarb Inków," ibid).

This is the first premise for looking for the Moon Cave or the Glassy Wall Tunnel in the Pieniny or the Levoča Mountains, but there is also the second one – well, in the latter, there are two towns with the strangely familiar (from Dr. Horák's report) names: Plavnica alias Plavnice and Stara L'ubovňa alias Lubocna.

Although there is no village called Ždiar alias Yzdar, (note, on the Polish side there is a mountain called Żdziar, which is located about 1 km south of Muszyna), but it can be Polish Żegiestów. No one took into account such a possibility. The name Yzdar appears in the English-language in Dr. Horák's report, and the fact that it is about Slovak Ždiar was a suggestion from the Czechs and Slovaks who investigated the matter.

The name Żegiestów has been distorted because the Anglo-Saxons tend to distort and shorten Slavic names and surnames. They are, to put it mildly, unassimilable. I would like to see an American pronouncing the name Żegiestów correctly. I can already hear those hissing and rasps, this "Zheghiestoff." Dr. Horák's story was translated several times, from Slovak to Czech, then to English, again to Czech and finally to Polish. Enough!? Such multiple translations are garbage, upon which many texts have lain down.

More than one Slovak probably lived with his daughters Anka and Olga in Żegiestów or nearby. He could have been called Slavek or Polonized Sławek or named Slavomir or Polish Sławomir. It is a borderland where both cultures permeate each other, like the land. After all, Poles still have their land in Slovakia today and vice-versa. Note, as has already been said here, Slavek didn't have to be a permanent resident of Ždiar but stay there temporarily with his daughters during the war or SNU. Therefore, you cannot place them in this area. This explains why seekers of the Moon Cave didn't come across the trail of Slavek, Hanka, nor Olga.

Writing his book about the glassy tunnel in Babia Góra, prof. Jan Pająk quotes the account of an individual named Vincenty, who came from one of the villages near Babia Góra. Most likely from Lipnica Wielka, Lipnica Mała, Zubrzyca or Sidzina (in which there are legends about mysterious tunnels in the slopes of the mountains, some of which lead supposedly to America, and certainly to Oravská Polhora). Because they lie on the southern slopes Babia Góra and near the border with Slovakia, ergo where it was easiest and quickest to reach the outlet of this glassy corridor. It is a bit surprising to me that Vincenty has revealed the secret of this tunnel because this kind of secrets in highlander families, especially when they are about treasures or even the so-called *spiski* - are kept the greatest secret and there is a conspiracy of silence. The question arises: why did Vincenty break this omertà law? The answer is one - he could do it because the outlet of the Glassy Wall Tunnel was destroyed in the mid-1940s by the Russians. How did this happen? Well, when writing a book about the V-7 weapon, during the collection of materials, we noticed that in the years 1945-46 in the region of Babia Góra there were Soviet soldiers claiming to be artillery workers making meteorological measurements. Is it not strange: artillery and meteorologists taking measurements on Babia Góra. This is nonsense. There were not many of them - 1 platoon - 30 - 40 soldiers. After completing the "measurements," they came down from the mountains burning the shelter on the south side of the Diablak peak dome and went to their people.

Now we understand what they were looking for and what "measurements" they were doing. They were looking for a tunnel with glassy walls just to destroy it and thus prevent escape from the Soviet occupation zone, of Nazi criminals and all those who had reason to escape this "paradise for working people of cities and villages," to America or anywhere else, and as I mentioned above, the NKVD and SMIERSZ knew exactly about the existence of this and other secrets from their colleagues from the Gestapo and SD, who in turn could extract them with torture from some Pole or Slovak who was unlucky to fall into their hands. After the war, local highlanders found the collapse of the outlet of the Glassy Wall Tunnel and decided that this could be told to someone from the outside. This is how the legend reached prof. Pająk. The rest we know.

The same could have happened with the Moon Cave, which is somewhere in the Slovak part of the Pieniny. Germans or Russians could reach it and find the treasure of Berzeviczy. In this case, the curse of the Incas priests could fall on the Nazis and/or Stalinists, with equal effect. Both totalitarian states have disappeared from the face of the Earth. We can only believe that these treasures are somewhere in the bosom of the Tatra Mountains, the Beskids or the Pieniny and are waiting for their explorer, who will take them and devote them to the restoration of the Inca Empire in Latin America.

CHAPTER 5

Dispute over Dr. Horák's identity

How it all began: adventurers, researchers, and ministerial officials - *You are wanted Captain Horák.* - Exploration in the field - Information by Eduard Piovarčy - Moon Cave as part of the intelligence game?

In the November and December issue of the Czech magazine "Fantasticka Fakta" in 1998, we published two extensive materials on the Moon Cave, as an example of a disturbing puzzle that a prehistory detective exploring Slovakia can come across (See: Jesenský M., Leśniakiewicz R.: "Tajemství Měsíční jeskyně," "Fantastická fakta," No. 11 (1998), p. 2-5, Leśniakiewicz R.: "Měsíční jeskyně. Další díl záhady," "Fantastická fakta," No. 12 (1998), p. 14-16).

After more than four years from the publication of these articles, the issues were enriched with a whole range of information obtained through the work of seekers like **Eduard Piovarčy**, from 1985-93 (Piovarči E.: "Správa o pátraní po osobách z príbehu" of Dr. Horák published in Americkom speleologickom spravodaji NSS News, 3/1965 from May 19, 1986, "Slovenská speleologická spoločnosť, Oblastná skupina nr 16, Terchová, Varín").

Two Czechs are considered the first seekers of the Moon Cave: Eng. I. Mackerli and M. Brumlik, who undertook their expedition to Slovakia on October 7-11, 1982, while the fact remains that already in 1981, on the order of the Ministry of Culture, a geologist and speleologist **Dr. Stanislav Pavlarčik** was looking for information about the Moon Cave (Pavlarčík S. : "Legenda alebo Skutočnosť?" "Ľubovnianske noviny," vol. 6, no. 49-50 (11/12/1980), p. 2). As for Slovakia, the first to get information from E. Piovarčy was the late speleologist and publicist, a researcher at the Museum of the Slovak Karst in Liptovský Mikuláš - **doc. Dr. Pavol Mittner**, who read the article by Dr. Antonin Horák already in 1976, courtesy of S. Pavlarčik.

Therefore, it cannot be excluded that the search began already in 1976 and was conducted by Slovak cavers, which no one published anything about. Six years later, Dr. Pavlarčik received a letter from the American **Frank Brownley** addressed to the Czechoslovak Ministry of Culture, which began the search under the program called "Records and documentation of karst and pseudacracial phenomena in the Pieniny, Lubowianska Wierchowina, Levoča, and Čergov Mountains," started on January 3, 1982. These activities were carried out with the assistance of the County Speleological Group in Spišská Belá. The report from this program, from 1982, contains a lot of data interesting from a geological point of view but it shows that there weren't found any material traces of the Moon Cave, and the data provided by Capt. Dr. Horák, regarding his fighting episode, couldn't be confirmed. Nobody responded to Dr. Pavlarčik's appeal in the local newspaper; no one remembered the battle fought by his unit at the place and time he had given. Is it normal for such a loss of memory among the participants of the Slovak National Uprising and also civilians? Dr. Pavlarčik himself rightly pointed out in our correspondence that *since the participants are silent, legends begin to arise.* The conclusions of his report are not only skeptical, but he adds to it, the case of the doppelganger of A. T. Horák, from Mníšek nad Popradom. This insurgent captain also fought in the area of Lubowianska Verkhovyna, and Dr. Pavlarčik managed to establish his true identity. According to the inhabitants of this village, this insurgent captain Antonin Horák was really called **Ernest Hönig**, who was the owner of the sawmill in this village. At the beginning of the war, he changed his name for racial reasons (he was a Jew). After the entry of German troops, he was hiding in the forest near the village of Medzibrod (part of Mníšek nad Popradom), where he had an underground hideout from which he conducted his entrepreneurial and partisan activity, which the local residents didn't like.

We will mention also about a handful of facts about the effects of further searches. Not only Dr. Pavlarčik after studying many historical works about the SNU and combat operations, but also other researchers didn't even find the mention of the unit that on October 20-23, 1944 would retreat to the region of Koš ice, and we found no trace of Capt. Dr. Horák - and we searched in all the archives of former Czechoslovakia and literature on SNU. The very identity of Dr. Horák is a great unknown and a great mystery. Engineer Mackerle, as well as other researchers of the issue, had only as much information about him as was apparent from the article in NSS News. Dr. Horák, as he claims, was indeed a linguist and, as he writes, he had a university education. Searching through the lists of university and other college graduates didn't give any results and Eng. Mackerle had to admit that A. Horák not only didn't obtain a doctorate but didn't even study a single semester at any philosophical or natural science faculty in the Czechoslovak Republic in 1920-1944. Already here his personality seems unreliable. Eng. Mackerle searching by correspondence in the US came to the fact that **Tony Horák** died in 1976, and of course, we will not learn anything from him. He also learned that Tony Horák had a restaurant in Pueblo, Colorado. He decided to look for his wife and descendants, but he failed again. What he failed in, his successors succeeded with. **Walter Pavliš and MA Ivo Hlásenský** – speleologists from Prague who have been dealing with this issue since 1994 – have done something in the Hussar style. They simply went to the USA and found the descendants of A. T. Horák, which became a breakthrough in the case. They obtained his death certificate and other information about his origin. Of course, they kept them secret, but on the Internet, you can read on their website (http://www.natur.cuni.cz/~karhu/jeskyne.htm) that even the search in his hometown didn't succeed, because, after his ancestors and him, there is not even a trace in the town. Even at the cemetery, there was no gravestone with this name.

The first field searches were conducted based on geographical data and coordinates given in the article in NSS News from 1965: 49o12'N - 020o17'E. S. Pavlarčik and I. Mackerle soon discovered that this data didn't come from Horák, but the editor-in-chief **Dr. George W. Moore**, who deduced it from Horák's characteristic landmarks. Pavlarčik's information shows that near the Siminy peak (1,289 m a.s.l.) the fact that the limestone layers were adjacent to the Paleogene sandstones (65-23 Ma ago) has not been confirmed. He conducted his research in the area indicated by the geographical coordinates given by NSS News, with the permission of the command of JW 1603 in Poprad. This is exactly what his report says. It so happened that the fanciful geographical coordinates given by the editor-in-chief of NSS News were in the military area of this JW 1603. That's why we thought for a long time that maybe it was part of some intelligence game - nay - the whole legend of the Moon Cave could be such a *крышей,* or *roof* or *cover* for some activities of the intelligence services of both Superpowers. When we realized that these coordinates were worthless, we began to search according to other tips given by Dr. Horák in his diary, and these were mentions of Ždiar, Plawnica, and Lubocnia, as well as of visited steep slopes of the Tatra mountains for the second time, where he looked for some signs on the surface of the rocks, caves and cave connections with the Moon Cave. Here, for the first and last time, he placed the Moon Cave on the steep slopes of the Tatra

Mountains, but can one seriously take his information for specific footholds? There are no others, and we have nothing else. Searching by I. Mackerli through the metrical records in Ždiar and paying special attention to people appearing in the text of the account: **Jurek, Slávek, Hanka, Oľga,** the grave of the **private Martin.** When no trace of them was found in the Ždiar area in the Belianske Tatras, we began to think again about the Low Tatras, in which SNU combat operations in Slovakia also took place.

In this search phase, E. Piovarčy was joined by the County Speleological Group from Terchová, which organized a field action on May 19, 1986, in Liptovská Teplička, near the Ždiar shelter, on the eastern slope of the Low Tatras. Our search for shepherd Slávek and his two daughters was also fruitless on the side of the Low Tatras near Hron, close to the village of Pohorelá. We reviewed the geological map and maps of the vegetation of this part of the Low Tatras, according to which it is possible to find a direct contact of the pine forest with a mugo pine, as well as a map of felling. We searched mainly in areas of limestone rocks, to no avail. No sign. Also, historically, there was no indication that the situation described in the diary took place there – there were no fights of retreating insurgent troops with Germans. The "Janošík" guerrilla unit operated in these areas. Persistent battles against the Nazis lasted from October 20th to 21st, 1944 on the southern side of the Low Tatras, in the area of Červená Skala and Telgárt. After October 26, the SNU ceased to exist and the soldiers switched to the guerrilla way of fighting. The problem was that in 1944, the first snow didn't fall until November 3. I. Mackerle, therefore, assumes that Dr. Horák's diary was inauthentic and was written in 1965, just before the article was published in NSS News, when the author had already forgotten some dates and data. That is why the exact date of the author's unit battle with Germans couldn't be determined. Therefore, only the facts remained: 184 men wading in deep snow, of which ⅓ were wounded and 16 on the stretchers, who were fired upon, on Saturday night from two German 70 mm guns, located on a close main mountain ridge, distant about 300 meters. Therefore, we had the view that it was not about the Low Tatras, but about the Belianske Tatras. Perhaps the snow fell a little earlier there. However, no such combat situation was recorded in the Belianske Tatras. The fights took place only in Lendak, where the guerrilla unit of Bielov-Kovalienka fought hard against the fascists on October 27, 1944. This unit in the strength of the company (about 100 soldiers) fought there for only one day, then its surviving part went to the Polish part and joined the forces of the Red Army.

In the first report of I. Mackerly from October 7-11, 1982, we found the interesting memories of the colonel **Tomáš Zamiška**, who claimed that he didn't know anything about the unit that about October 22, 1944, withdrew eastwards through the Levoča Mountains. It was the worst period of the SNU, all insurgent forces headed for the Low Tatras and joined the partisans. It is unbelievable that someone would go in the opposite direction - i.e. to the east, but it cannot be ruled out, because it could have been a group of people from eastern Slovakia who were returning home in a military way, and an officer could be its leader. So, there was still some alternative.

In the second half of the 90s of the last century, a group of residents of Žilina joined the search for the Moon Cave for a short period of time, and was headed by **Eng. Gustav Skřivánek**, who in 1997 published several articles about his search in Mníšek XXXnd Popradom and Stará Ľubovňa. It is noteworthy that he also heard that: *This insurgent captain wasn't named Anton Horák, but Honig (Hönig) or Horning (Hörning), and was the owner of large wine cellars, and that there were such fighters who were partisans at night and collaborated with the Germans during the day. Personally, however, I think (writes Eng. Skřivánek) that such information is deliberately disseminated so that people lose the desire to search for the Moon Cave.*

This mysterious double, of Capt. Horák is such Old Maid in our game of the Moon Cave mystery. Nobody holds this card for long. It could rip the whole matter off its romance, or is it fear of MOSSAD? Anyway, we must accept this mysterious person who ominously emerged from the gray-black war, the insurgent past of the village of Mníšek nad Popradom, like a ghost, but this German Jew Hönig can't be not accepted. People in Mníšek nad Popradom still remember him well to this day (Skřivánek G.: "Mesačná šachta," "UFO magazín," No. 9 (1997), p. 21, see also No. 8 (1997), p. 21 and 31). His nickname "Captain Horák" covers exactly with the name of the author of the article in "NSS News" about the Moon Cave. In Kežmarok, Stará Ľubovňa and also in Mníšek nad Popradom, Skřivánek was looking for one of the wounded soldiers, who was supposed to live there and whom Horák remembers as Jurek. In a brief information, you can read that the search group met in Kežmarok a man who talked to Jurek and promised him that the next day would lead him to the Moon Cave. The other day, the man canceled everything and didn't even want to talk about it (Skřivánek G.: "Mesačná šachta," UFO magazín, No. 8 (1997), p. 21). It is similar to the story of S. Pavlarčik, about how he once encountered a person in a restaurant in Mníšek nad Popradom, who promised to show him letters that were sent to that person from Palestine by Ernest Hönig aka Anton Horák. The mysterious interlocutor on the second day canceled everything and didn't appear for the appointment. Such events are really remarkable and puzzling. It seems that during the war more than one tragedy took place here with the participation of Hönig-Horák and people prefer not to tell about it - persons who are looking for traces of Horák's identity. It would follow from the fact that this Hönig-Horák has a twisted insurgent past, which is still alive in the memory of the inhabitants of Mníšek nad Popradom and surrounding towns. Note, it should also be mentioned that Skřivánek in Kežmarok learned that the Moon Cave was sought by numerous seekers, including Americans.

It seems that the mystery of the dual identity of Hönig-Horák is to be solved because he could be the "inside man," "ratter" of the Gestapo in the resistance movement - which was simple for the Germans, because as an influential Jew he could easily be drummed up by them under threat of extermination – and *de facto* he carried out orders not from the SNU command, but from Berlin. Such things happened everywhere in the Nazi-occupied Europe, because Jews – which is not spoken of at all now – also cooperated with the Nazi occupiers against the population of countries, in which they lived, and after the Soviet army entered, they collaborated with the second occupier. After the war, he fled to the West and, as a Jew, left for Israel. He was afraid that the Slovaks would hand him over as a collaborator of the German authorities, so he tried - as you can see, successfully, to intimidate them. Therefore, there is a possibility that in the whole case is involved, among others Israeli military intelligence – notorious MOSSAD - which, after revealing his past, gave him an offer he couldn't refuse. That's where alleged Americans in Slovakia came from, but more on that later in the report.

The catalyst for further research activity was the response to research results posted on the website of Prague speleologist Walter Pavliš, MA. In Prague, a working meeting of Piovarče and Pavlarčik took place, where they exchanged their results. During the confrontation of their archives and accurate maps of the selected regions, they located several high-altitude artillery positions and associated them with artificially created caverns – miniature caves – which, as Dr. Pavlarčik found out, were manned by German crews from September 1944 to January 1945. There were two such locations on the main ridge of the Belianske Tatras. This discovery automatically brought the next question to the debate, whether Horák's unit was fired upon from these positions during the crossing of the main ridge. In this context, once again considering the text of Horák, Dr. Piovarči came across a weighty but neglected fact. There are many versions of Czech and Slovak translations of Horák's article, but they are all inaccurate. Thanks to this, we all were influenced by this 12-hour fight during the withdrawal of the unit. So, it should not be: *Keeping our positions for 12 hours, I decided to order a retreat from the skirmish.* The idea was that the unit remained in position for 12 hours, and then there was a skirmish as a result of which Horák ordered a retreat. There was no regular battle lasting half a day.

Most likely, Horák's unit was attacked during the crossing of the ridge of the Belianske Tatras by an artillery unit with 70 mm guns, firing from a distance of 300 meters. Perhaps they wanted to get out of the German encirclement eastwards toward Košice and for this, they had to cross the ridge of the Belianske Tatras because the valley communication routes were already manned by the Germans at that time.

Pavlišov thus led to the fourth search for the Moon Cave in the Stará Ľubovňa county, the results of which he acquainted the public on June 30, 1999, on the TV program entitled "Klekánice" broadcast by the Czech television channel ČT-1. The exploration group worked in the Osieh Vrh area - 859 m a.s.l. in the vicinity of Malý Lipník. The cave in which they worked didn't have the structure and character described in Horák's diary. Neither the letters "A.H," the initials of the author of the Moon Cave account, nor the six scratches symbolizing the six days spent there, were found there, let alone the date. The geological structure of the cave also doesn't match the description of the geological structure of the Moon Cave. The only noteworthy mention was that Pavliš's group contacted the descendants of A. T. Horák in Slovakia or the Czech Republic, because he met him personally and convinced him that his story should have been taken completely seriously.

Is the case of the Moon Cave just a fragment of an intelligence and counterintelligence game in which the account of the late A. T. Horák is used to? This option cannot be completely excluded (See: www.quest.cz/moonshaft). Walter Pavliš points out that Horák published an article about the Moon Cave only in a specialized scientific magazine, proving that its source is serious and the whole course of events has a real factual basis. For this researcher, it was also noteworthy to discover that Jacques Bergier had the author's permission to cite his article, and therefore, it is possible that Bergier had close contacts with the author. It is a pity that Bergier died in 1978, which ruled out any possibility of verifying this information.

Contrary to the fact that all Horák's notes sound unbelievable, some places in his story raise a lot of questions and doubts. Is it possible, then, that shepherd Slávek brought his only daughters to the soldiers in the cave in such a complex war situation? It seems that the idea of exposing two young girls to such a risk was not very rational. After all, as Horák writes, they kept watch throughout the night and didn't want to stick their noses out of the cave so as not to come across enemy patrols on skis. Horák claims that Jurek got to Košice within six days. From the area of the Low Tatras, this distance is about 90 km as the crow flies, which means that you had to go through the mountainous terrain, bristling with enemy patrols and guards about 110-120 km. Could they cover this distance in winter, after snowfall, only at night, and for six days? The area of Stará Ľubovňa is slightly closer to Košice. 80 km as the crow flies. These remarks are not so suspicious, but they raise doubts. Horák's plan was to travel 10 km a day, so the Moon Cave was about 60 km from Košice as the crow flies. This distance roughly corresponds to the center of the Levoča Mountains. It looks as if Horák intentionally placed his adventure location near the intersection of geographical coordinates, which dreamed up (or got from a school atlas) the editor-in-chief of "NSS News," and then he wrote to the journal about the steep slopes of the Tatra Mountains and the shepherd from Ždiar.

The next contentious point is the pine torches, with which Horák illuminated the cave during its exploration. He also used a carbide lamp. I wonder what technique he used to make them. He burnt a lot of these torches. The pine bough alone will not burn, and if so, only for a moment. Everyone who spends free time in the countryside knows how to prepare a torch from what is at hand. Into a pine log split across, dry resinous twigs and resin are put, and of the latter, it is needed a lot for the torch to burn for 15-20 minutes. Making a torch alone takes a lot of time and the most collecting resin. Horák does not describe how he prepared them; they are as obvious to him as us an electric lamp. According to what shepherd brought to the wounded soldiers during his six visits, it would be excluded that Capt. Horák could make torches of material, oil, etc. – because every bite of the material was during this harsh winter and in a cold cave needed to wrap himself in it. The use of many torches, as described by the author, seems simply impossible, due to the lack of material for their preparation, and also because of the difficult situation in which three wounded insurgents found themselves. Making a torch requires time, material, and two healthy hands. Capt. Horák was wounded in the left arm with a bayonet and a bullet, which implies a significant limitation of freedom of action. Unless he found the necessary materials in the cave, but he doesn't mention a word, because it didn't occur to him that someone would be making a problem of it after many years?

So, it's amazing that the wounded Horák was able to penetrate the cave, corridors, underground tunnels and chambers unknown to him, completely alone. Something like this indicates that, in addition to courage, this man also had a developed sense of orientation in the underground and was able to move in it, and the description of how he went through the individual parts of the cave indicates an experienced speleologist because he is realistic and convincing. That's how it could really happen. The situation was as it was and basically, everything was possible. It is interesting that Jurek wasn't surprised when Horák disappeared for long hours and without telling where he was going. Caring for two wounded soldiers should have ordered him, as a commander, officer and the most efficient of the three, to stay with them most of the time. Just carrying firewood had to take a lot of time and strength, and not only for torches but also for heating of the inhospitable and cold cave rooms. However, there is some explanation for this problem, which is discussed later in this report. It is also strange that insurgent soldiers cooked food in German helmets. It's like drinking water from the shoe of a fallen enemy. If the Slovak soldiers didn't have their helmets, which is quite strange in the described combat situation, the soldiers still had canteens. So, how did it happen that they boiled water in German helmets, which they ripped off killed Germans or found during the attack on German trenches? This is strange, first Horák describes that they got into the crossfire of two 70-mm guns, and then writes about the attack on German infantry - but he was hit on the head with a butt, and then he was wounded with a bayonet and a rifle bullet in his left hand. So, all this action looks quite unbelievable. According to the war logic and tactics of battle, the infantry sits in the trenches as long as their own artillery shoots in order not to get hit by fragments of their own grenades, and rushes to attack after the artillery preparation.

Let's return to the hypothesis that the Moon Cave is part of the intelligence game. Of course, this is possible, because Western intelligence was interested in Czechoslovakia during the Cold War. Let's not forget that in this country there were training centers for terrorists from Arab countries, which were run by specialists from the Soviet KGB and Czechoslovakia Št.B. (Czechoslovakian equivalent of the Soviet KGB, Polish SB, Hungarian AVH, East German STASI, Romanian SECURITATE or Bulgarian Državna Sigurnosti). The Belianske Tatras was a military training ground for high-mountain infantry and commandos from airborne troops. The troops of the Northern Group of Soviet Forces were stationed in the ČSSR in Liptovský Mikuláš – they were rocket forces, and who knows if space. Operational rocket-nuclear weapons were probably also stored there, which like in the case of Poland, was not even known to the highest party and state authorities of the ČSSR. (Cf. Leśniakiewicz R. - "Raport: Ufologia i ekologia - Polskie doświadczenia" - paper for the II International Ufological Conference, Budapest, February 13, 2000 - see http://ufo.internauci.pl).

These areas were worked out by the CIA, which was easy because they were extremely touristic areas. Mention of the activities of Ernest Hönig aka Cpt. Anton Horák suggests that the Israeli MOSSAD was also interested in this area and the Moon Cave. Therefore, this area was certainly protected by counterintelligence services of the Soviet KGB and GRU and additionally by counterintelligence services Št. B. and in the border zone, by the operational services of OOŠH (Czechoslovakian equivalent of BPT). Each of these organizations ran their own object matter in a secure area, whose threads led to Prague and Moscow. That is why we think that we would learn the most about the Moon Cave, not so much in the military and counterintelligence archives of Bratislava and Prague, but in Moscow - in Lubyanka – KGB, and Chodynka - GRU, from where some part certainly permeated to the West - to Langley, London, and Beersheba. Let's not forget that the Cold War lasted and every point of the advantage over the opponent was worth its weight in gold or uranium, and this was expected to be found in the Moon Cave. This, or technology straight from the Platonic Empire of Atlantis.

CHAPTER 6

New search horizons

Nota spaelologica - More questions than answers - Again Belianske Tatras? - From the research journal of Walter Pavliš and Ivo Hlásenský - A letter from Piotr Parahuz - Searching in insurgent history: fake twins and secret Nazi research - Dr. Horák really existed.

Horák's alibi, catching animals and bats, wasn't a very convincing excuse to visit the cave for hours and secretly. The thought of eating baked bats may turn our stomachs, but in this situation, you can eat everything, including leather shoes and earthworms. However, the wounded soldiers, already the next day – after the provision of food by Slavek – weren't in such a difficult situation. So, they didn't have to indulge in baked bats. In addition, it is difficult to suppose that Horák kept all this secret and didn't tell about it his comrades of misery and struggle. Keeping it secret in such a stressful situation was unbelievable. At the time, the means to survive were at the highest price, and not even the greatest secrets of the depths of the mysterious cave - weren't they? Didn't the shots fired in the cave to the blue-black wall surprised Jurek? If he didn't hear them, it would mean that the cave was either deep or vast. The map of the Moon Cave published in books and magazines proves that it consists of huge chambers and corridors 6-10 m high. The width of the sidewalk in front of the mysterious shaft reaches 20 m, and its height is 7 m, as well as its length. If Horák was telling the truth, it would mean that we are dealing with the entire cave system in the area. The biggest caves are breathing. Through the bottom holes, they draw in cool air, which heats up passing through the system of chambers and corridors, and then flies out through the upper holes. This is how it is in the so-called active caves thanks to this ice is rare in them throughout the year. The situation is different in the case of passive caves, in which ice lies under stagnant frosty air for years. Passive caves usually have the form of wells with one hole, while active ones have several holes of high deterioration. If the cave were so extensive that Jurek didn't hear the shots fired in its distant parts, it would be obvious that at its opening, as the description implies, one could feel a penetrating, intense draft that would either draw air into or throw air from the mountain massif. There is not a word about this phenomenon in the author's notes. If they camped at the bottom of the cave, smoke from the fire would have been consumed by the cave. If, however, at the upper one, they would feel a warm breeze that would throw smoke from the cave outside, and insurgents could thus be noticed by the Germans. The description shows that the cave was in the high parts of the mountains, which logically indicates that there must have been warm air in winter. It is interesting that the notes don't mention it. The increased humidity that occurs when the air flows out of the cave would give them a hard time on cold days.

From the description of the unit skirmish, it is clear that the cave is located at a high altitude above sea level. Over the range of the subalpine forest - i.e. 1,200-1,500 m a.s.l. – as evidenced by the presence of mountain pine (Pinus montana), which is mentioned in the journal. But then we found further contradictions in his notes. High mountain and mountain caves are characterized by a large number of branches, unevenness, narrowing, and gaps. The author, writing about his 1.5 hours wandering around the Moon Cave, never once mentions this kind of obstacle but only about the narrow gap before entering the mysterious crescent shaft. This is a great inconsistency from which there is no appeal. Meandering caves with slight deterioration are found under mountains up to 900 m above sea level - like Demänovská Caves. Very rarely such horizontally stretched caves are found at higher altitudes - an example is the Cave of Dead Bats near Ďumbierom in the Low Tatras. But also, in this case, there are even, horizontally located corridors and chambers, separated by chimneys, siphons, and corridors that create an amazing karst maze. It is his 90 minutes journey that may indicate that the cave was at least half a kilometer long, and therefore such a vast cave system couldn't hide from the inquisitiveness of speleologists for a long time. .

When we take a better look at the situation and think whether a vast cave system not yet discovered could be located in the area of the Belianske Tatras, Levoča Mountains or somewhere north of Stará Ľubovňa, or north-east from Ždiar, we'll come to the conclusion, no. No, it is because there are no limestones near the Levoča Montains. The only thick layers of limestone are found only in the Belianske Tatras, and a small limestone island can be found west of Stará Ľubovňa, while quite small limestone islands are located in the border range, just north of it. A limestone island west of Stará Ľubovňa, according to geologists E. Mazúr and J. Jakàl, is a poorly developed type of karst and combined scree-layered structures (Mazur E. - Jakál J. : "Typologické členenie krasových oblastí na Slovensku," "Slovenský kras," vol. 7 (1967), p. 5). Islets of limestone north-east from Stará Ľubovňa, according to these authors, belong to a poorly developed karst structure. In other words, there couldn't be any caves. Unless the Moon Cave is an artificial creation, which after thousands of years became similar to a cave. We will come back to this thought later in the report.

This situation accurately and unambiguously limits the search field of the Moon Cave. Thus, only a small limestone island remained near Stará Ľubovňa and a thicker limestone nappe in the Belianske Tatras.

The Belianske Tatras (Belianske Tatry) belong to the most extensive karst terrains with an area of 25 km^2. They are built of dolomites and Triassic and Cretaceous limestones of various types, belonging to the Križnian nappe. There is developed high-mountain karst in the Muráň limestones of Havran - 2,154 m a.s.l. and Predné Jatky with escarpments and karst cavities. It seems, and this is indicated by Horák's records, that his unit was fired upon from artillery positions from under Hlúpy vrch (Crazy Peak) - 2,061 m a.s.l. (Remains of these artillery positions have been found - see Pavlarčík S.: "Kaverny vysokohorského palebného postavenia pod Hlúpym vrchom v Belianskych Tatrách," "Spravodaj Slovenskej speleologickej spoločnosti," vol. 27, No. 2 (1996), p. 14-15). The most important for us is the fact that in the slopes of Bujačí vrch - 1,947 m a.s.l., at an altitude of 1,390 m, there is located the longest cave in this high-mountain karst - 300 m long Alabaster Cave, which is a remnant of some larger cave system. This circumstance suggests that at high altitudes (1,200-1,400 m) large horizontal cave systems may have once existed. Near Alabaster Cave, at an altitude of 1,440 m, there is the second cave, Ľadovy sklep (pivnica) 50 m long, and on the slope of Muráň - 1,890 m, at an altitude of 1,559 m, Muránska Cave 60 m long. On Crazy Peak, at an altitude of 1,996 m above sea level, there is the through Kamzičá cave 13 m deep. In addition, there is known, more than 200 m deep Tristárska jaskyňa (priepast) in the Havran massif, available for tourists, 1,752 m long Belianska cave. Recently, many new caves and wells were discovered in Nový vrch - 1,999 m a.s.l., and if Horák's journal was real, then indeed his cave could be located somewhere *on the very steep slopes of the Tatra Mountains*. This is shown in the further part of his diary:

Probably thanks to a large amount of fresh snow, threatening avalanches and enemy patrols on skis, Slavek will not get to us within a few days.

Avalanches certainly couldn't threaten on the forested and rounded slopes of the Levoča Mountains, with their highest peak Ihla - 1,281 m above sea level, in L'ubochnianska vrchovina with the highest peak Kraczonik - 974 m a.s.l. on the Polish side of the border, or in the area of the Spiš Magura - lying vis-à-vis the Belianske Tatras - with the highest peaks Priehrštie - 1,209 m a.s.l. or Veterný vrch - 1,122 m, which is proof that the author locates the Moon Cave at higher altitudes. This is also evidenced by the existence of the shepherd Slavek from Ždiar, but at the same time, the names of *Plavnica* and *Lubocnia* contradict this. Is it possible that they were also made up by the editor-in-chief of NSS News? It would appear so, because they aren't in Horák's diary, but in the supplement written by Dr. Moore. According to Dr. Pavlarčik, locating the Moon Cave in the Belianske Tatras is pointless and historically undocumented and unproven. He assumes that new caves may still be found in the Belianske Tatras, which is possible in the last unexplored karst area of Slovakia, but these discoveries would have nothing to do with Horák's account. There may be abyssal cave systems connected by horizontal corridors, in which a man without technical protection can't count on 90-minute walks.

We can also continue our reflection on doubts as to whether Slavek and his ancestors explored the cave to this level, as Horák did. People from this period had neither the courage nor the time to meticulously penetrate the caves, explore the dangerous world of the underground, from which they had no use, and in which – according to their legends and stories – were supposed to be, monsters, dragons, and demons from hell, as well as poisonous gases. If Slavek had known about the Moon Cave, he would have passed on his knowledge to posterity, and would not have taken the secret to the grave. Horák hoped that Slavek didn't have a son and the daughters would get married in the nearby villages. Slavek's descendants today would know well what to do with this secret and how to use it.

However, we think that this conclusion is too hasty, as the mountain people penetrated all caves in the Tatras and the surrounding mountain ranges in search of treasures and ores as well as precious and semi-precious gems. After all, there was a whole branch of literature describing the underground worlds of the Tatras, Karkonosze, Beskids and even the Świętokrzyskie Mountains – the so-called "spiski" – from which it was possible to find out where the treasures or ores were and how they could be excavated. Slavek's descendants would certainly not announce that they know the location of the Moon Cave. This is not the kind of people who, for sensation would lose shelter, that could be useful for example, for war. This is not this kind of mentality.

It is likely that Horák didn't want this cave to be discovered without him. The mysterious words in his diary prove this:

Then I put this proof in the crescent-shaped shaft, on the ash torch. Perhaps it will stay there long until this mysterious structure disappears completely behind the veil of stalactites and stalagmites. Slavek has no son to entrust the secret of the cave, his daughters don't know it, and yet they will get married in other villages. So, if I don't go back and explore this cave, nobody will see it in a few decades.

Hmmm...there is something illogical in these words, after all, the daughters were in the Moon Cave, so they had to remember the way to it and pass the knowledge to their children, or Slavek, who could also pass the family secret not to his son, because he didn't have him, but to the grandchildren, he might have had. Well, unless both daughters also had only daughters.

The author seems to knew that he wouldn't return to this mysterious shaft. But how could he know that then? After all, he was a captain and had his combat merits, which could give him hope that after the war, he could still be needed in the republic in which he could stay and be useful to the world of science by discovering this mysterious artifact for it. But from the explorer's point of view, it has no logic, because every explorer would do anything to return to his discovery. On the contrary, if Capt. Horák had been a collaborator of the Nazis or Tiso supporters, he would have been skeptical of the possibility of his return to Slovakia. Even if he wrote or recreated his notes in 1965, it is strange that he didn't trust that his descendants would return to the cave.

Suppose Horák is right and such an artifact actually exists in the Slovak mountains. In this case, finding the Moon Cave according to his data is simply impossible. What should we look for? First of all, for information about Horák's identity and past, because he is the only real person from the whole event. This is the only sensible thing that can lead to the specific point, and we can say that it was successful. Each researcher has done a great job. So far, no trace of the insurgent captain Horák has been found in the military archives throughout Czechoslovakia, just like shepherd Slavek and his two daughters, as well as Jurek and Martin. Walter Pavliš is closest to solving the puzzle, because he came across the trail of Horák's descendants and got a lot of interesting information from them, and he can get more information, which their father might have left to them.

Let's return to the mysterious double of Capt. Horák – Ernest Hönig, a Slovak citizen of Jewish origin who changed his name at the beginning of the war for racial reasons. In Mníšek nad Popradom, he had his sawmill, and shortly after the entry of German troops, he was hiding in the forest near Medzibrod, where he had a perfectly masked hideout, from where he managed his industrial and "partisan" activities. These actions, however, were not identical to the aims and intentions of the Resistance Movement, because Horák did what he liked. At night he was a partisan in the mountains, while at daytime he was a

Gestapo confident. He belonged to this type of partisans who robbed and killed anyone who got in their way. As you can see, this is an extremely dark figure, and quite accurately contradicts the stereotype of a poor, persecuted Jew, corresponding to the image of a common bandit. It is not known what other sins he had on his conscience. In addition, he had an illegitimate child in Mníšek nad Popradom. This fact is proof for doubters, of his existence. He hid until the end of January 1945, i.e. the entry of Soviet troops, from which he fled to Palestine. He had to have a lot on his conscience that he was afraid to stay in Slovakia, and his "guerrilla fame" could bring him a lot of trouble. In Palestine, his escape ended. From Palestine, Horák sent letters to Mníšek nad Popradom, to a woman with whom he had a child. The last such letter showed that A. T. Horák was killed by an Arab captive in a prison camp where he was a guard. His path officially ends here; but it's not so obvious. There are spicy stories about him, that went beyond the frame of Pavlarčik's account, and which we have from conversations with him. At that time, when his account was being formed, such details could not be noted in it.

At the moment, we find it useful to devote some space to the studies of Walter Pavliš and Ivo Hlásenské already mentioned here, and this is because their achievements are surrounded by a fog of mystery. From time to time, some shreds of information about them come to the public, although in the case of the Moon Cave, there are not so few of it.

They first encountered information about the Moon Cave in November 1994, when they read about it in the Speleo magazine. The next information is from Walter Pavliš's website - http://quest.cz/moonshaft.

Autumn 1994

- We read the article by Dr. Horák in the Speleo magazine;

- November 25 - we are looking for the author's name in the registers of the Faculty of Linguistics at the Charles University in Prague - no results.
- Next week, attempts to get the original text from NSS News, which was briefly translated to Czech. It turned out that the text in "Speleo" was some sort of samizdat and further searches didn't bring any results. A visit to the SNU Fighters' Union file didn't bring any new information except that there was some miner Antonin Horák from Ostrava who had nothing to do with the discoverer of the Moon Cave. Also, the file of the Národná obroda daily and searches at the Military Museum didn't bring any results.
- Next week, you will be getting a copy of the English-language text in NSS News at the office of the Czech Speleological Society. We discover some facts that have been removed from the Czech edition.

Winter 1994/95

- Visit to Slovakia, field inspection, document review.

Spring 1995

- We gain access to geophysical search capabilities, accurate aerial and satellite maps of the area, and access to geological data of the area of our interest.
- Contact with Eng. Iven Mackerly and review of his archive.

Summer 1995

- Another trip to Slovakia - searching in caves in selected places. Eight new caves and one chasm have been found. Visits to museums, document review, etc.

Autumn 1995

- Search in archives.
- Studying sources on the resistance movement in Czechoslovakia and Poland.
- Consultation with a psychologist to determine the mental profile of the diary's author and the degree of his truthfulness.
- Onomastic examination of names in Slovakia for compliance with Dr. Horak's writings.
- Searching at the Military Museum, Charles University and the Ministry of the Interior – no results.

Winter 1995/96

- Search in the Military Archives - Antonin Horák was found, but it was only his namesake.
- Visit to the US embassy.
- Obtaining accurate geological maps of interesting locations in Slovakia.

Spring 1996

- Internet searches.

Summer 1996

- Internet searches.

- Trip to Slovakia and searching selected areas, talks with museologists.

Autumn 1996

- Contact with close relative of Dr. Horák in the USA. New threads are emerging from the life of the insurgent captain.
- Search in the Ministry of the Interior and the Municipal Archives in the probable place of residence of Dr. Horák before World War II.

Spring 1997

- Finding Dr. Horak's death certificate. Finally, we obtained basic data on the date of birth and death and personal data of his parents and spouse.
- Further searches in the Ministry of the Interior archive and postal archive.

Summer 1997

- Telephone contact with relatives of Dr. Horák in the US, further information about his life and activities.
- Trip to Slovakia, searching in well-known places, discovering a new passage in a known cavern.

Summer 1998

- Local vision in the selected location. Without success.

Spring and summer 1999

- Contact with an informant who in 1971 talked about the Moon Cave in Colorado. The authenticity of the journals was confirmed. Some of them were published in NSS News, and their fragments relate to a mysterious metal walls shaft in Slovakia.

April 2000

- Obtaining further documents of Dr. Horák - commercial papers and private letters without any mention of the Moon Cave.

The latest news on this site is dated April 18, 2000, which didn't surprise or worry us - we were already stuck in a whirlwind of events that were gathering pace.

When on October 11, 2002, we were adding up the results of our investigations at home, we received an email from Mr. **Piotr Parachuz** from Canada, in which he reported about the local, i.e. American, investigators of the Moon Cave case. We quote it with some abbreviations irrelevant to its content:

Dear Mr. Robert,

I'm Piotr Parachuz from Canada. [...] I have just read articles on the Moon Cave on the CBUFOiZA website. This story is almost identical to the one I heard on the local radio in December 2001, and which interested me a lot [...].

This broadcast, of December 29, 2001, was an interview with Ted Phillips, who is an American researcher of physical remains of UFOs. In 1970, somewhere in the USA, he met a 72-year-old Czech geologist who was in the army in 1944 and described a story almost identical to Antonin Horák's, which was reported by Dr. Miloš Jesenský. Unfortunately, Phillips gives neither names nor places, because, as he said later, he had to act in secret due to the intelligence activities of the government of the great state, whose name he didn't give, but probably it's Russia, going in the same direction since 1981.

Phillips said that he was on a trip in Central Europe in April 2001 and after 3 months of searching he found the entrance to this cave. He didn't say where exactly it was, but showed photos probably from the Belianske Tatras, below the boundary of the subalpine forest. In the corridor of the cave, he also found scraped initials of three military men from 1944. After entering the cave, Phillips walked along the corridor for almost 200 meters, where the rock was collapsed. He said the corridor could be seen further, but the rocks were uncertain and may have collapsed, so he didn't go on. He was to come there later in 2002, with the right equipment and try to pass.

The entrance to the cave is about 750 m below the top of the mountain, and about 100 m from the place, where in 1944, a Soviet aircraft crashed. In this place there is a monument to this accident, which was caused by strange reasons – the entire on-board electrical and electronic installation went off. Ted Phillips says he has a map made by this Czech geologist. When he went on the surface of the earth along the corridors, he reached an area where, according to the map, there was supposed to be the entrance to this crescent object – I mean, he was above it – and it was a magnetically strange area the size of a small room. Inside this area, the instruments behaved abnormally. The electromagnetic field strength meter jumped up every two seconds, and the compass also pulsed at 0.5 Hz.

Best regards.

Piotr Parachuz

This letter was a kind of breakthrough and since then things went with a flourish. Again, the information gathered during our search for Nazi secret weapons of mass destruction in the godforsaken places of the former General Government in 1943-44 was useful to us.

Today, these are areas covering part of the Sucha and Nowy Targ counties, and the most prominent point of this area is Babia Góra - the Queen of the Beskids - towering over the area at 1,725 m a.s.l. This is an amazing land. Orawa bulwark from the north, and from the south the gate to Lesser Poland. Roads leading to Silesia, Slovakia, and Hungary, as well as to Cracow and Przemyśl via Nowy Sącz cross here. This land is shrouded in legends about dragons, robber thalers, uncounted treasures accumulated by devils in the holes in Diablak, and the newer ones - about the Agarthan tunnel in Babia Góra, Nazi experiments on the Krowiarki Pass, mysterious bunkers in Grzechynia, and Soviet search for uranium ore in Osieliec and Żarnówka.

The enchantment of Hitler with occultism and secret knowledge certainly didn't push him to drill rocks and build underground shelters in the Karkonosze, the Owl Mountains, and among others also in the Beskids. (See Ribadeau-Dumas F. - Tajemne zapiski Magów Hitlera," Warsaw 1992; Jesenský M., Leśniakiewicz R. - WUNDERLAND: Pozaziemskie technologie Trzeciej Rzeszy," Ústi nad Labem 1998, Warsaw 2001.) The mystery of the V-7 weapon, to which we devoted our book, as well as work on the Nazi bomb A, H and D has its continuation in the complex of bunkers buried after World War II, and which were built by Germans, Italians, Ukrainians, and Poles - whereby all except Germans, were forced to work by the Nazis - in Grzechynia, in 1943-45 - until the entry of the Soviet army.

There are few living witnesses of what the Germans did in Grzechynia, Osielec, Żarnówka and on the Krowiarki Pass. Our interviews with a Home Army soldier and a resident of Jordanów - Tadeusz Łukawski, who during the war was sent to work in the Der Riese complex in the Oberwiesegiesdorf area (today Głuszyca Górna) and a resident of Sucha Beskidzka, Józef

Mędrala, indicates that these two constructions - the one from the Owl Mountains and another from Grzechynia have several points in common. These similarities include:

1. Both constructions were carried out in difficult terrain conditions - in the mountains.
2. Both constructions were carried out by concentration camp prisoners and captives.
3. German and Italian engineers were employed in the construction.
4. The guards were soldiers from the SS formation, and later soldiers of the Wehrmacht.
5. Both constructions were located in places that were not on the way of the attack of Polish and Soviet troops.
6. Both construction sites were near important communication routes.
7. Both constructions were located in close proximity to science and research centers (Wrocław, Prague, Cracow).
8. Uranium deposits were nearby or sought.

While the matter of the Der Riese complex is clear, the matter of the bunkers in Grzechynia requires investigation. Tadeusz Łukawski claimed that during the war, the Nazis conducted an intensive search for molybdenum and manganese ores - both elements are used to give the steel elasticity, corrosion resistance, and hardness.

Józef Mędrala claimed that uranium in Żarnówka was not sought until the post-war years and the search was discontinued in the 1960s. It was carried out by Poles. Traces of drilling devices were found near the Przysłop Pass. Perhaps there is some truth in it because the geological structures of this part of the Beskids are similar to those of the Czech Jáchymov in the Ore Mountains, where uraninite deposits are really located.

In addition, he claimed that the Grzechynia bunkers had too little cubature to put any factories in them and served only for defense purposes.

But what were they supposed to defend? Probably not a miserable, dirt road from Maków Podhalański to Stryszawa and Sucha Beskidzka? The most logical seems to be the explanation that these bunkers were supposed to defend access to some research complex in the future – who knows whether regarding the A bomb or the rocket V-7 *Haunebu - Vril* rocket discoplans in the Jałowiec Range. The similarity between the geographical conditions of the Owl Mountains and the Jałowiecki Range is striking: they are not high (Jałowiec measures 1,110 m a.s.l. and Wielka Sowa 1,015 m a.s.l.) and are located in the vicinity of small settlements. Interestingly, Grzechynia was near the geometric center of the territories of the Third Reich, which means that at the then range of heavy bomber aviation, it was virtually impossible to be bombed by the flotilla of Allied bombers – perfect place: deep facilities, peace, silence, wonderful landscapes, sun-filled mountains, rich forests, and clean water streams. Idyll as in Sleeping Beauty – as Peenemünde was called, before HRVA of the **General Walter Dornberger and SS-Sturmbahnführer Prof. Dr. Wernehr von Braun** was created there. It was in this idyll that the German weapon A was to be forged, and maybe even now? Although it might be as well the N bomb that could be made from what the Nazis possessed, or other weapons from "the land of dreams" of the then Nibelungs. By the way, many things indicate that the infamous V-7 was not an atmospheric or space vehicle but was supposed to move primarily in time - as discussed in the next volumes from the series "WUNDERLAND." (Leśniakiewicz R. - WUNDERLAND 2 - Hitlerowskie rakiety Stalinab," Jordanów 2001 [script]; Leśniakiewicz R. - WUNDERLAND 3 - Mały Apokryfb," Jordanów 2004 [script]).

During World War II, the Germans conducted intensive searches in the Babia Góra region, including by the soldiers of the

Grenzschutz and Gebirgsjägerregiment and scholars who carried out experiments on the Krowiarki Pass with the progenitor of the V-3 supergun - known under the code names *Hochdrückpumpe*, *Schnelle Elise* or *Tausendfüßler* - with a caliber of only 5 incl=hes or 127 mm. Attempts with such a supergun were also carried out simultaneously on the island of Wolin. It was possible to determine with the help of the **reserve ensign Jerzy Archacki** from Zakopane, who heard about these tests in the 1960s while serving in the BPT Watch Tower in Lipnica Wielka, as well as TOPR and GOPR rescuers from Zakopane and Nowy Targ. Its caliber was small, but the gun had a practical range of 50 - 55 km, and Hitler intended to use it to shell London from the French town of Epperleques on the English Channel. The basis for these experiments was the village of Grzechynia, in which the Germans built several bunkers of unknown destination in 1942-43.

Note, similar searches were carried out by the Germans, as we know from our Hungarian colleagues. Also, in the Domica-Baradla cave complex in the Slovak Karst, Aggteleki Nemzeti Park on the Slovak-Hungarian border. They were looking there for the entrances to mythical Agartha. Did they find it? We don't know. It is known, however, that shortly after the war the shelter on the southern slope of Diablak was taken by a dozen Soviet soldiers who claimed to be artillerymen and said that on Babia Góra they were doing . weather observations. Strange - isn't it? After some time, they descended into the valley, previously having burned the shelter, and in 1947, went to the Soviet Union. What were they really doing there? Nobody knows. I have first-hand information about German and Soviet actions from surviving witnesses living in Lipnica Wielka and Zubrzyca Górna, who remember the shooting in 1942-43 and searching in the mountains - supposedly for Polish and Slovak partisans, but actually, it is not known for what. This is also information from soldiers from intelligence cells of the Home Army from Zakopane. We can add to this the stories of people from

Jordanów, Maków Podhalański, and Grzechynia who still remember the works in Grzechynia. Few know that Germans in 1942 conducted an intensive search for uranium, thorium, manganese, titanium, and molybdenum ores in the vicinity of Jordanów, Osielec, Bystra Podhalańska, Sidzina, Żarnówka, and Zawoja.

As you can see, legends (really only legends?) are like tied up ropes - one results from the other. However, at the stage of our investigation, we could already say something for certain. At the beginning of 2003, we managed to make contact with **Ted Phillips**, who sent us copies of documents confirming the reality of the existence of Dr. Antonin - not Anton - Horák. He was not Slovak but Czech. A copy of his resume, which he had to write to the French authorities while asking for asylum shows that:

- He was born on July 7, 1897, in Hermannsstadt (Transsylvania, Austria-Hungary); parents: **Karel Horák** and **Maria née Cooker**;
- In 1903-07, he studied at an elementary school in Karlín, Prague (Czech Republic);
- In 1907-15, he studied at a high school in Karlín, Prague and spent his holidays and learned languages in Paris and London;
- In 1915, he passed the secondary school-leaving examination;
- In the years 1915-18, he served in the Austro-Hungarian Army. In 1916 he entered the reserve as a First Lieutenant;
- In the years 1918-19, he served as a First Lt. of the CS Army, stationed in Slovakia and participated in battles with the Bolshevik Hungarian army of Beli Kun;
- In the years 1919 - 21, he studied at the Mining Academy in Banská Štiavnica.

- On October 11, 1921, he was awarded the title of mining engineer by MA in Banská Štiavnica;
- In the years 1921-25, he worked as an engineer in the salt mine in Visakna (Transsylvania);
- In 1925, he leaves for a six-month stay in the USA, where he visits mines;
- In 1925-26, he completed postgraduate studies at the Special School of Geophysics at the University of Prague
- In the years 1926-30, he worked as an acting director of the mine in Příbram (Czech Republic);
- In 1930-31, he left for the USA, Argentina, Canada, and Mexico to visit mines;
- In 1932 - 33, he worked as technical director at the Visakna salt mine;
- In the years 1935 - 39, he worked as the director of the mine in Banska Bystrica;
- In 1939-41, he was arrested by the Germans, sent to KL Theimwald, from which he escaped on July 22, 1941;
- In the years 1941 - 43, he was hiding in Slovakia;
- In 1943-44, he participates in the Resistance Movement and the SNU in Carpathian Ruthenia;
- In February 1945, he became the director of the Visakna mine [under Soviet occupation];
- At the end of May 1945, he returned to Prague;
- At the end of 1945, he filled the post of the mining advisor in the government of Czechoslovakia;
- In December 1946, he became the head of the Special Sector for Jáhymov at the Ministry of Mining of Czechoslovakia;
- On March 7, 1948, he was dismissed from his post;
- In June 1948, he escaped to France.

From the above resume, it would appear that it was an escape from Soviet communists who came to power in Czechoslovakia after the assassination of President R. Masaryk.

This resume also shows that the communist authorities of the ČSSR had a reason for the disappearance of the memory of the man who fled west with all the atomic secrets of the Czech and Slovak as well as Hungarian and Polish uranium mines. As you know, after July 16, 1945, uranium and its ores became a strategic raw material primarily for the construction of atomic bombs. The Soviet authorities began exploiting uranium-thorium ores in their occupation zone of Europe, to have their own supply of this raw material, and so that it wouldn't be owned by countries that were subordinated to the Kremlin as a result of the Tehran, Yalta, and Potsdam agreements. This accurately explains the veil of secrecy around this character and the activity of Western intelligence and Eastern counterintelligence around the matter of the Moon Cave. Indeed, both thought that they were dealing with some unexplored uranium-thorium ore deposit that could give several hundred tons of this valuable raw material. Hence, the case of the "second Horák," which became the perfect legend masking the real Dr. Horák – the discoverer of the Moon Cave – which over the years has been replaced by a common bandit using the lawlessness to get rich. Who knows if Dr. Horák later worked for the CIA and was therefore cursed by the communist authorities? This hypothesis is also acceptable because he knew many secrets related to mining in three countries: the Czech Republic, Slovakia and Hungary, and in addition probably also Romania and Poland. In this context, one can understand why Bergier in 1963 classified the extremely important facts from Dr. Horak's diary, namely his contacts with Jewish resistance organizations in Poland and the Czech Republic. An organization such as ŻOB (Jewish Combat Organization) and Dror operated in Poland (specifically in the General Government) after the fall of the Warsaw Uprising, i.e. from October 1944, while the youth of Hechaluts operated in the Protectorate of Bohemia and Moravia. The reader will find detailed information on this subject on the websites of the Simon Wiesenthal Institute in Vienna [page: Simon Wiesenthal Center Multimedia Center Online - 08623 - YMBOHEMIA_JW.htm] and the Adam Mickiewicz Institute in Warsaw [page: www.iam.pl). Also, our conversations with witnesses of those days - **editor Andrzej Zalewski** from EURO-EKO-RADIO PR-1 in Warsaw and **Józef Durek** from Jordanów, partly confirmed the fact of operating Jewish partisan units in southern Poland. He deliberately omitted this information, because he was aware of what could happen when the ČSSR communists put their hands on this artifact, and thus their "big red brothers" from the USSR. It is obvious that he didn't want to give the communists an additional trump card that could be used against the free world. It was shortly after the Cuban crisis (October 1962) and communism was dangerous. Very dangerous. The Cold War was just beginning, and the technology race fueled by it was gathering pace.

Further materials obtained from Ted Phillips showed that the Moon Cave is located in an area bounded by the towns of Stará Ľubovňa and Plaveč in the south, on the north side of the border and Muszyna, Żegiestów and Piwniczna in the north - on the Polish side. Also, everything is correct: the geological structure of this region confirms the observations from Dr. Horák's diary - in two places on the tertiary sedimentary formations of the Carpathian Flysch, there are two "caps" of limestone rocks from the Jurassic and Cretaceous – one in the west of the area, the other almost in its center. This is where the Moon Cave should be.

It is also interesting that on the Polish side of the border there is a mountain called Pusta (empty) - 1,050 m a.s.l. - rising between Muszyna and Krynica. So, are there also underground spaces in it and the surrounding mountains that the inhabitants of these areas knew about since they called it that? Such caves are really there.

CHAPTER 7

From Nazi scholars to NKVD agents

A small encouragement to start with: a strange photograph of Robert - *Retaliation weapons* under Diablak - Christmas Eve in Luboń - What did the tank wreck hide? - Interview with a witness of those days - Views of Maciej Kuczyński and two reports on underground spaces.

Already when we were working on this book, a very long April-May May long weekend, rest or dog days allowed Robert to move from home here and there and look around. Unfortunately, what he saw in the forests of the Jordanian region didn't fill him with optimism, but quite the opposite. Mass felling of trees by wood thieves, fire lanes rutted by tractors in places where there should have been animate and inanimate nature reserves. It saddened the fact that at the crash site of the AN-24 PLL LOT plane of flight number LO-165, which got completely destroyed below the summit of Polica on April 2, 1969, there is no plaque or even an ordinary cross to commemorate this event. Yet it was the first great catastrophe in the history of Polish civil aviation. After all, this is history, and with the capital "H" - not to mention the fact that we should somehow honor these 53 victims of this catastrophe, including **Prof. Dr. Zenon Klemensiewicz**, from whose name is derived the name of the local Upper Subalpine Forest Reserve.

And here the first interesting thing: on May 1, 2002, he visited with his children the summit of Polica (1,369 m a.s.l.). The weather was great – the sun was shining, the sky was cloudless, but the wind from the south was strong – the mountain wind, which was cold at first, and then, when it had swept the cold layers of air from above Nowy Targ and the surrounding area, it became very warm. From the south one could admire the toothed saw of the snowy peaks of the Tatra Mountains, from Roháče in the west to Spišská Magura in the east. From the north, there was a wide view of Lesser Poland and part of Upper Silesia. On the last climb to the summit of Polica, Robert took the picture of his kids. To his amazement, in the positive, he saw the silhouette of something that he certainly didn't notice during photographing. This object that captured his *canon* is definitely neither an airplane nor a balloon or helicopter. The direction indicates that it hung above the main peak of Babia Góra - Diablak, so in the place where, according to local folk tales and legends, there should be a tunnel system leading to Agartha.

But not only, because talking to the inhabitants of Bystra Podhalańska and Sidzina, he learned that all this area was riddled with tunnels leading to the Slovak side, and some of them were built already in the 14th and 15th centuries by the miners from Wieliczka and Bochnia salt mines. In the forests, there were mysterious stones reminiscent of the elements from which the pyramids were built, of size 2x2x2 m. What were built with them or what they were used for – no one knows now. Anyway, these legends are still alive and circulate in the villages near Babia Góra .

On May 3, 2002, I received an e-mail from the well-known Warsaw nestor of Polish ufology, Mr. **Kazimierz Bzowski** - a former Home Army platoon leader-cadet fighting in the Warsaw Uprising, who already after the war got to know a lot of information about the Nazi secret weapons V - and who in his letter describes the following events:

[.] Recently you wrote about Lubon Wielki. It so happens that I know it even from the days when there was no shelter. As a child, I spent holidays 9 times in Rabka-Grzebieniówka, close to the place where the roads from Skomielna Biała to Rabka and Limanowa meet - in 1931-39 . I remember the pre-war tourist map, which was on a large street board in Rabka-Zdrój. There, on the slope of Mount Szczebel, the entrance to the cave was marked. The same entrance was on the old military maps of the Austro-Hungarian Army. It is not marked anywhere on Polish post-war maps, even military ones, because in December 1944 this entrance was blown up by the Home Army guerrilla unit.

It was later said that "the unit went out of the encirclement through the tunnel." Even before the war, the news was that this tunnel led from the entrance on Szczebel to Mszana Dolna. I was in July 1963 on the pass near Szczebel. I was looking there for this blown up passage, but everything was overgrown with forest, then in 1972, I was in Luboń for the last time. Judging by the descriptions of the "Tunnel to Mszana Dolna," it is highly likely that this is the same tunnel as under Babia Góra, about which Dr. Jan Pająk wrote. It is worth looking for this entrance on the old maps.

In his next electronic letter of May 4, Mr. Bzowski supplements this information as follows:

I still remember from the last two pre-war years, when I went to Luboń a few times, a tourists' conversation about this tunnel in Szczebel. In 1939 I was 14 years old and I didn't dare to go there alone. After the war, in 1962 and 1963, also during several expeditions to Luboń, and in the company of the highlanders from Rabka, which owned part of the forests in Luboń, I heard from them that the "unit of Węglarz escaped from the hunt in December 1944 through some tunnel in Szczebel." The conclusion is that this is not about a cave in Szczebel, but about something completely different = one more mystery of these mountains.

Have you heard anything about the German tank, which in the winter of 1945 was escaping from the area occupied by the Russians, on the Luboń ridge, from the west, i.e. from Jordanow, and plunged into the woods in such a place that neither turn back nor go further, and it stayed there forever?

On September 20, 1972, I went with Stanisław Łopata from Rabka to the slope of Luboń to his own forest to collect saffron milk cups, which apparently grew a lot there. It was so foggy in the forest that we couldn't see the end of our outstretched arms. We circled blindly through the woods and got on the rusted remains of some armored vehicle. Because of the fog, yellow and thick as pea soup, we couldn't even determine where it was or even what it was, but it looked like it was torn apart by an internal explosion. In the end, we came across a riverbed and went down southward along its course.

From all this, it would follow that this tank lies somewhere on the western slope of Luboń Wielki (1.022 m), below its ridge connecting it with Lubon Mały (869 m), near the hamlet of Krzysie (Surówka - 860 m).

A few days later, another electronic letter came from Mr. Bzowski, in which he described another event of his lush youth, related to Luboń:

After the Warsaw Uprising, I didn't go into captivity. After many adventures, I was in Cracow already 6 days after leaving Warsaw. There I contacted the local AK. Once in a conversation, I said that I know the area around Luboń and Gorce.

A few days before Christmas Eve 1944, I was offered to go there as a liaison to the Węglarz's unit. We set the date for the night from 24 to 25 December, when the Germans are less vigilant. It wasn't an "order" because I wasn't subject to them, but a "proposal." I was to deliver an envelope wrapped on a Russian concussion grenade and stuck with a medical adhesive and, if necessary, detonate the grenade. The whole was placed in a "stale" loaf of wholewheat "card" bread, cleverly crafted with the grenade inside. What German would crave for such miserable bread if there was any check on the train? I took the passenger train to Chabówka, from there on foot to the intersection of the road from Skomielna to Rabka. About three hundred meters from this intersection, going in the direction of Skomielna, on the right side there is the guest house "Gozdawa." It was known to me before the war, because its owners, Ms. Janicka and Wiśniewska, knew my family. These ladies were completely surprised when I came to them on Christmas Eve with the "password."

There I got a white camouflage coat with a hood and skis, greenish with a white longitudinal stripe, typical for German alpine shooters, also a sketch on a piece of paper showing where to go, with marked indicative points visible at night, especially during the full moon. I left at around 6 pm. First, I walked straight up in the open, then turned right. I crossed the stream and walked along the mixed terrain, a lot of forest and some glades covered with snow. From below, from Rabka there could be heard the singing of "Stille Nacht." (German Christmas carol).

I was walking for over an hour and a half and from the denser forest, my path went out into a fairly large clearing, very brightly lit by the moonlight. I was standing in the thicket on the edge of the forest for a long time, observing the area and listening. Nothing, complete silence and no sign of some life. When a small cloud covered the moon, I went to this plain. For a few minutes, I was only hearing a weak "stroke" of my own skis in the snow. The moon came out from behind the clouds and almost immediately as if someone had torn a thick canvas, a tercotle, typical of German MG could be heard. The echo went through the woods and I threw myself to the ground with my nose in the snow, spreading my legs with skis sideways in the shape of the widely open letter "V."

Waiting again for another cloud to cover the moon. Now, bending my right leg with the ski flat on the snow and throwing the left one, I moved left sideways to get closer to the wall of the forest I had just left.

The moon came out of the clouds again. A long pause motionless...The moon hid behind the cloud again. Now, I pulled both legs together and ran down the slope – to the right, towards the wall of the forest. Violent rattling behind me and I saw a bunch of light green bullets that flashed left of me, over the place where I had gotten down before, but I had already fallen into the shelter of trees. Stepping back a few dozen meters, I watched the clearing again. Unfortunately, without binoculars, I couldn't see where these SS-bastards were sitting.

It couldn't be helped. I knew that I wouldn't reach my destination. Further path would be suicide. I came to the edge of the forest when the thick cloud covered the moon and it got dark. I bent the open ends of the grenade pin, pulled it out, and with all my strength threw the grenade as far as possible towards the Germans. A powerful echo of the explosion flew through the mountains.

On December 26th in the evening, I was back in Cracow. There I learned that my path was unnecessary. The unit hadn't been around Luboń or Szczebel for several days. All they knew was that; it wasn't known where they went. By the way, it was the strangest Christmas Eve in my life.

We didn't encounter eighter of the stories, which obviously doesn't prove that it didn't take place. In the guidebooks about the Beskids of **Władysław Krygowski** and the latest one of Pascal, there is not a word about the "Tunnel in Szczebel," and they only describe the Cold Hole Cave in the slope of this mountain. I also asked my relatives about the history of the tank, but nobody remembered that this would have happened in the winter (January or February) of 1945. This story is all the strange, because if they were Nazis, why were they fleeing in a tank, and not walking around the Soviet and Polish outposts in the forest, heading west or southwest, and not east. Maybe some German survivors captured the Soviet tank and tried to escape into the forest, but why exactly on Luboń, which is the highest peak in the area??? Admittedly, Kazimierz Bzowski suggested that if it was possible to go onto Luboń Wielki on *Junak*, then it would be also possible in a tank. Nay. The Nazis got onto Elbrus in their *beemers*, but it's one thing on a hundred-liter motorcycle and it's another thing in a multi-ton tank. You can go to Luboń Wielki in an off-road car also from Rabka-Zaryta and from Skomielna Biała because there are ways used to deliver food and leading to shelter and TV relays, but again, a light all-terrain vehicle with a powerful engine is not a 25-30-ton tank. Even if a German decided to go to this mountain from the west, he didn't go far, even if he was following the present-day blue trail from Jordanów, because the rapidly increasing steepness of the slopes of Luboń Mały would have quickly stopped him in the Czerniawa Forest or the plowlands of Skomielna Biała. Alternatively, he could fall into one of the branches of the Jama Stream or Luboń Stream and definitively bury himself in the soaked ground. In that case, I would agree with Mr. Bzowski, but only in that case. Even modern tanks wouldn't be able to overcome such a steep slope, and the reader needs to know that the slopes of the Island Beskids are the steepest slopes of the Beskid – apart from the northern bluffs of Babia Góra, of course.

Well, it can be assumed that there was a method in this madness, and these refugees were not as stupid as they looked. They drove a tank to the slopes of Luboń because maybe it was from there that could take them the Nazi flying saucer – the V-7

Vril disco plan. Maybe they were some Nazi VIPs who, surprised by the Russians, didn't want to fall into their hands. What did they have to hide? Perhaps the documents and other artifacts related to the mysterious installations of "V" weapon on the Krowiarki Pass and in Grzechynia; and no one saw them? Well, because there was no one, Poles living in the area hid from Germans and Russians, so nobody wanted to go outside, because nobody would risk their lives unnecessarily.

There is another possibility, namely, that the Nazis wanted to break out of the encirclement because the Russians were walking from Rabka-Zdrój and from Łętownia, i.e. from the south-east and the east. In the area of today's Jordanów Wrzosy Estate on Flakówka, there was a sharp exchange of fire with the Germans who carried out actions delaying this march of Soviet troops. Perhaps it was then that this lonely tank rally took place, which ended on the slope of Luboń Wielki. I wonder what this tank was carrying. Maybe Wehrmacht or Gestapo documentation? Or maybe something related to research on the "V" weapon carried out in the vicinity of Grzechynia near Maków Podhalański? This could be the case and it cannot be ruled out. I gave this riddle to the **editor Bogusław Wołoszański** and his "Club of sensations of the 20th century." In any case, this story is still unexplained. There was probably nothing left after the tank because if it was torn apart by an explosion, the local peasants probably took it to some junkyard and it ended up in an open-hearth furnace – after all, it was several dozen tons of nice iron. On Luboń there is another place of a mysterious catastrophe from the 1960s when the Czechoslovak *Mi-2* helicopter crashed there in a thick fog with two Czechs on board. This disaster has not been fully explained.

Note, at the peak of Luboń, there is also a small cave which you can reach following the Borkowski steep mountain path – trail no. 7 (yellow signs) in Pascal's guide or route no. 26 in

Krygowski's one – and located at position: 49°38'59"N – 019°59'50"E.

Speaking of caves, I decided to investigate this matter of the tunnel in Szczebel or Strzebl (977 m), which is the second version of the name of this mountain. In its slope at position 49°41'44"N – 020°00'30"E there is the Cold Hole cave (Cold Grot), whose total length of corridors is 25 m. Its name comes from the fact that even in summer there is low temperature and it is the only cave glacier in the Beskids. So, this proves that from the Cold Hole (470 m) there is no secret passage or hidden corridor, otherwise, the ice would be melted quickly by the air circulating there. You can reach it by following routes 1 and 2 described in the Pascal guide mentioned here, or roads 33 and 34 in the Krygowski's one. This cave was explored on May 25, 1835 by **Ludwik Zejszner.** And it was certainly placed on all tourist and military maps of the Szczebel massif, there is no doubt about it. At that time, the name Strzebel was used even on maps of the Austro-Hungarian Army.

In the Beskids, there are legends about secret underground tunnels and passages built by miners from Wieliczka or treasure hunters from the Brotherhood of St. Lawrence, also known as the Brotherhood of the Seven Stars, and all that to find gold, silver, precious stones and other less valuable ores. The sandstone outcrops themselves make an amazing impression and I'm not surprised that people, looking at the sometimes fantastic shapes of rock snowmen, began to come up with different legends – because what the eye couldn't see, the imagination added. Although in this respect the Beskids are far from the Karkonosze, exactly the same mechanism works here: fatigue caused by climbing or descending a steep and difficult slope (and Szczebel is one of the steepest mountains in the Beskids in general.), unrestrained imagination, excitement with adventure, specific lighting conditions. It's enough for a man to see something unusual in every pile of stones.

On the other hand, these piles of stones don't have to be accidental and there is a possibility that in these mountains there are caves, tunnels, corridors and underground passages, which even the local population doesn't know about, and even if it does, they are not eager to share this knowledge with *low-landers*, because, why should they? So, Mr. Bzowski's story may be true, at least in part. Where would these tunnels come from? I don't believe much in the relations of prof. Pająk, that aliens or other "almighty creatures" from the depths of our planet would make them. For me, the most probable is the hypothesis about some Supercivilization from 20,000 years ago, whose buildings, or rather what remains of them after the Great Conflict of the Gods-Astronauts, are still in front of our eyes, but we treat them as something normal, because we look at them from birth, and that's why it's so hard for us to acknowledge it. I haven't found the tunnel, but it may be anywhere else.

It is only a part of what awaits us in the Beskids and other places in our country. The problem is that we choked on the world and we don't see what we have on our doorstep, and the biggest secrets are usually at your fingertips.

Robert managed to find a man in Jordanów who remembers those times. He is a 90-year-old Home Army sergeant Józef **Durek**, who in 1942-45 fought in the ranks of the unit commanded by Capt. "Leopard" in the Beskids and Gorce.

On June 5, 2002, he interviewed him about what was happening in the Jordanów region during the last days of the war and shortly after the Soviet army had entered. This interview is interesting because it sheds some light on the events in the vicinity of Jordanów on the last days of the rule of the Third Reich in these areas:

Question: Do you know anything about this mysterious tunnel from Mr. Bzowski's story?

Answer: No, I don't know anything. I've read the story, but I can't tell you anything about it. I don't know this case. I don't know at all. I don't know anything about it.

Q: Do you know anything about this tank or tanks?
A: Nothing too. In the camp (base of partisans of the "Lampart" unit) I was the head of our 10th company. I took part in expeditions to Slovakia, Bia ła, Frydman, the fight for Ochotnica, a major skirmish in Rdzawka, where Janik was seriously wounded. And my job as ahead of the company on the spot, guard service, etc., and exercises with the youth who first encountered the weapon. It was in November when I found myself in this area. I got heart problems and articular rheumatism and that was the end of my soldiering. I had to withdraw from that area. Then there was the demobilization of the regiment, and the threat from the Soviet partisan group from Zolotar's unit continued to increase.

Q: Who were these people, these Russians?
A: First, it was Alosha Petrov, who led the group, and then, in September, Zolotar who was a member of the NKVD working in Poland. When the Soviets were approaching, he worked on the liquidation of the AK soldiers, from the 27th Division of the Home Army in Volhynia and was thrown here for the same purpose. In the first days, we worked together – joint attacks on the enemy and fights for Ochotnica. But as the Red Army advanced, this cooperation took on different colors. Our commander "Borowy" prohibited them from robbing our Polish and local people, and our command undertook to provide them with food. And they received it many times. Once they got 5 head of cattle from the food warehouse they occupied. But that wasn't enough. Anyway, later, during a certain action in Mszana Dolna, "Borowy" with his group was attacked by the Soviet unit and got wounded. That's why it was such a job.

Q: I would like to know whether during the war and shortly thereafter, in 1945-47, the Russians were looking for something here?
A: No, our Department of Security was looking for a commander of the 3rd regiment of Podhale riflemen "Harnasie" in the area. And they looked everywhere.

Q: Did the Russians after the war look for German specialists in the field of secret weapons?
A: No, no.

Q: I'm asking because, during the war, Germans conducted research on secret weapons – e.g. they were shooting from Krowiarki Pass at the Tatras from the V-3 guns, and in Grzechynia a band of bunkers was built, and it's unknown what they were supposed to defend.
A: Of course, there were such attempts. And at our place, behind the train station in Jordanów, where today there is the Cracow Works "Armatura," there were preparations for the production of nuclear weapons. This news was published in RWE and this way it came to us. And there it was also said who of our people from Jordanów worked there, to avoid them. It was RWE who gave the message.

Q: When was that?
A: It was for sure in the 1950s or the 1960s.

Q: Were there any military warehouses? At least that's what my parents told me, and I remember it myself when I was little.
A: There was the production of parts for nuclear weapons, where today is "Armatura." They then liquidated it, because as you understand, when such a message spread, it had to be moved somewhere.

Q: And it was for the Russians?

A: Only. For sure. We didn't have nuclear weapons. [.]

Q: How long have the NKVD Russians worked there?
A: Russians used to visit there in 1945, but in 1946 already not.

Q: Were those of the NKVD ferreting about for uranium ore in 1945-46?
A: No, there was no such thing here in the Jordanów region. Although no, wait, wait – as I taught in Osielec in 1947-48, I learned that in one of the houses in Kamieniec between Bystra and Osielec, the NKVD started a boiler. They were looking for some VIP from the underground, specifically from the Government of Exiles in London. They didn't catch anyone, but the NKVD murdered the livestock of these people and injured them themselves. To this day, it is not known who the Soviet Security Service in Kamieniec was waiting for.

That's all from Józef Durek. As you can see, the Beskids hide many secrets from our recent history. Who was the mysterious "guest from London?" What was stored around the Jordanów railway station? Nobody will answer these questions unless we find some traces in the archives of the former Ministry of Public Security, Ministry of National Defense, or Ministry of Interior.

Now something different, but also related to the underground voids under the Beskids.

In May 2003, after a series of publications of the famous Polish traveler and writer Maciej Kuczyński, in the "Gwiazdy mówią" weekly, about the planetary underground in Afghanistan and other Asian countries, I asked him to comment on information about the Moon Cave and other formations of this kind, such as the Glassy Wall Tunnel described by Dr. Jan Pająk. Here is what he told me in his email of May 25, 2003:

Mr. Robert.

[.] You are asking me what I think about it (the Moon Cave). You have touched on many aspects, from Shambala to UFOs, etc. but I would like to refer only to what an alleged eyewitness wrote about the Slovak Moon Cave. I myself was in hundreds of limestone and sandstone caves on several continents and started exploring the Tatra caves and also numerous Slovak ones (I have my own discoveries in Belanska Jaskynia). I also wrote hundreds of descriptions of caves in books, the press, in various reports as well as scientific papers. From this point of view, in the description of the Moon Cave I don't see a single element, detail or clue that would indicate that the author was in anything other than a natural Slovak cave, hollowed in limestone in the course of a normal, already well-studied karst process. This applies not only to the shape of corridors, crevices, wells, underground chimneys, but also to the infiltrative forms of calcite, or crystalline calcium carbonate, colored in the caves by oxides of various metals and minerals. There is a place for snow-white or cream "porcelain," which is difficult to scratch with a knife, and for black (manganese oxides), flexible "rubber" (a plastic form of calcium carbonate called milk of lime). "The tower of the castle covered with "dripstones" is an obvious, typical powerful stalagmite. "Fissure walls covered with jags" is a common picture of the chemical dissolution of limestone by CO2 saturated water. "The trough in yellow sandstone" is a dry bed of a cave stream with a typical cave clay deposit that remains after the chemical breakdown of limestone. "Limestone bottom" is almost the "manipulation" of the author of the description. Indeed, the cave corridors are lined with limestone, but by nature. The whole description is a typical impression of a man, a bit scared, who was in a cave for the first time. At the same time, everything seems to him larger and more extensive than it really is, although many corridors, also in Slovak caves, are the size of subway tunnels and have halls big like cathedrals, and their mazes developed on many levels, connected by wells, stretch over a dozen or several dozen km.

In my opinion, the described cave really exists, but it is a completely natural creation of nature. As for its length, the author of the description probably exaggerated: an hour and a half of the march deep into the mountain and a return after the torch and candle go out is unbelievable! All the rest, about the participation of intelligent beings in the formation of the cave, is evidently added to this story, only on the basis that something seemed unusual to the young guerrilla. This is really not enough to make such far-reaching hypotheses.

The second story described by Dr. Pająk is pure fantasy or a fairy tale. Although no one has seen it, because the testimony of an unspecified person is no proof, whole concepts of underground tunnels of global scope are built on this, although this contradicts geological logic. First of all, such tunnels would be constantly collapsed and blocked by tectonic movements or closed by the pressure of the orogen. They would also have to overcome the moving contact points of drifting continental plates, Secondly – they would be flooded with water bad that's why, for example, pump stations are still operating in each mine.

Finally, it is difficult to explain why 20 thousand years ago, when the Earth was extremely sparsely populated, someone powerful, possessing "cosmic" technology, would have struggled to build tunnels under the oceans, instead of sailing or flying over them? But this leads us to completely different considerations.

Generally, although I assume all hypotheses are probable until I check them myself, I think, in the case of caves, that there are only small shafts, tunnels and wells carved out by people. All the vast mazes in the world (except mines) are natural.

What I could, i.e. what was located by the authors (e.g. Daeniken – South American caves), I visited myself and always found that the author had no idea what he was writing about. It always turned out that it was about natural creations, and their richness of forms could significantly confuse the layman.

Maciej Kuczyński

Well, he is a man to which we take our hats off, because we only read or heard about many things, and he was there. Anyway, you don't become a member of *The Explorers Club* in New York on somebody's say-so. Däniken's criticism is correct here because we ourselves don't always agree with him. The theory of visits of newcomers from space has its serious disadvantages, and the hypothesis of ancient Supercivilizations, which explains the vast majority of anomalies observed, is much more adequate.

And one more voice in the discussion – this time from Podkarpacie:

Also, in May 2003, the coordinator of the Subcarpathian Branch of CBUFOiZA, Mr. Arkadiusz Miazga sent us two interesting accounts about strange underground constructions about which there are legends in the Podkarpackie province, and here they are:

Report on the alleged underground tunnels located in Subcarpathia in the village of Pstrągowa, told by Kazimierz Skworzec on March 3, 2003, in Będzienica

The following story was heard by Mr. Kazimierz as a small boy from his grandfather. It could have been in the 1940s. Strange tunnels were supposed to be discovered several years before the outbreak of World War I in 1914, in the village of Pstrągowa.

The people there were digging a well for water. Mr. Kazimierz said that about seven concretes deep, which means that it was about 5-6 meters underground.

When the well was dug, it was slowly filling up with water, but after a few days it turned out that the water was gone and the well was empty, which surprised the inhabitants a lot. They decided to check what could be the reason for the disappearance of water.

According to Kazimierz Skworzec, they allegedly dug up and enlarged the well and rappelled down.

It turned out that there was a crack at the bottom through which water was apparently escaping. People's curiosity turned out to be stronger and it was decided to deepen the hole to see what is under the bottom of the well. Two people who dared to descend the lowest with the lamps said that there was a semicircular tunnel. Its size also had to be significant because Mr. Kazimierz said that there could have easily gone a horse-drawn cart.

Apparently, it wasn't just one tunnel because a little further there were others. Unfortunately, Mr. Kazimierz remembers nothing more than the story he heard in his childhood from his grandfather. It is not known what happened to the well. Most likely it was buried.

We have heard that in Pstrągowa there are still places on the earth that are characterized by great depth. Some threw stones through small gaps, listening after what time it would fall. Unfortunately, it is not known where these types of cracks are, because no one knows it, but only heard about them.

Perhaps in the above case, it is about the famous "glassy tunnels."

Sleeping knights near Subcarpathia.

In Podkarpackie Voivodeship there is one more premise that may indicate the existence of underground tunnels. It is the legend of sleeping knights. Fragments of this legend come from the book "Ziemia Gorlicka na tle legend" written by Anna and Tadeusz Pabis in 2000.

"The fact that inside the Salomon Mountain in Biecz lies a sleeping army, it was known in Biecz and the surrounding area for as long as the legend existed. Well, under the former castle of Saint

Jadwiga there are asleep, armored from head to foot knights. According to legend, they are young, handsome, neither aging nor dying men. From the eastern side, next to the through road from Gorlice to Biecz, at the foot of the Castle Mountain, there is an iron door leading to the basements, and in ancient times this entrance led deeper into this mountain and then through the tunnel to the city of Biecz. Once a daredevil went with a torch deeper into the underground, where he noticed a huge chamber with a sleeping army in it. The brave man, despite his courage, stood rooted. He got scared and started running away. He accidentally hit a protruding stone that made a lot of noise. One of the vigilant knights then asked:

"Brother, is it time yet?"

"No, it's not time yet, sleep peacefully," said the frightened daredevil.

In later years, this entrance was walled up for fear of tunnel collapse. But at the top of the hill, there was a deep hole and when in Biecz a dangerous plague raged, the dead were thrown into this pit and then the hole was cluttered and filled with soil."

This is all the information about this interesting legend.

Arkadiusz Miazga
CBUFOiZA-Podkarpacie

CHAPTER 8

Secret of the Orava Beskids

Strange phenomena over Magura and mysterious lights on the slopes - Bottomless pit, missing people, thunder without storms for the second time - Arrivals from the night sky - About the meteorite transformed into hoes and plowshares - The topic returns: Strange discovery on Červené vrchy.

This story has some reference to the Moon Cave matter. The author of this account, **Augustín Víťaz**, described a story that corresponds with both Dr. Pająk's account of the Tunnel in Babia Góra and Dr. Horák's account. This story is so unusual that it cannot be bypassed by writing about the secrets of the Slovak mountains. And here is this interesting material.

(Víťaz A. : "Magurská záhada," "UFO magazín," vol. 12, No. 2 (2003), p. 13-15).

Also, in Slovakia there are still places where human legs rarely enter. One such area is the Orava Beskids mountain range on the Slovak-Polish border. Even today, the northern part is inhabited extremely rarely, and in dense forests, there is peace and quiet. And it was here, that almost 200 years ago strange events described below took place.

In the nineteenth century, the area of the Orava Beskids was a land forgotten by God in which the devil had just said "good night." Small villages and human settlements sat on the slopes of the mountains and in the valleys. In one - today quite forgotten settlement - during an autumn a whole series of unusual phenomena was observed, the news of which spread only verbally, and nobody wrote them, and still they have survived to this day. As for me, I heard about them in the mid-1960s, from the couple, whose ancestors lived near the peak of Magura - 1,018 m a.s.l. (This mountain is located between the hamlets of Pientakov Ral and Vyšný Koniec - at 49°31'N - 019°22'56"E.) Today it is very difficult to determine the credibility of this story because the details come not from the second and third, but from the tenth hand. They told, however, what they heard from their parents, and those from theirs, etc. After so many years from these events, it is extremely difficult to separate the real nucleus from the legends that over time have enveloped it. Therefore, one should approach these stories with a dose of reserve and comparing them with legends from various parts of the world will allow us to see that these are not just stories made up by simple villagers.

It is difficult to determine the date of the beginning of mysterious events, actually it is impossible. Based on this story, one can only calculate that these events took place in the autumn, most likely before the revolutionary year 1848. 1813 appears to be the most probable, but it is neither certain nor provable.

It all started on a certain autumn late afternoon. The weather was nasty - the foul weather lasted for several days, so that everything was soaked, and the sky was leaden. Shortly after sunset, the inhabitants of the settlement found a strange anxiety of livestock. Piglets were restlessly banging around in a pigpen, the cows were moaning nervously, the dogs continued to snarl and walked around the backyard with hair bristled at the nape of the neck. People didn't attribute any importance to this until the animal behavior was related to what happened at night.

Shortly after dark, it ceased to drizzle, the wind stopped, and there was stony silence in the village. The villagers heard the roaring of swollen mountain streams that had never been heard before. The voices carried far away, and every step sounded like an elephant pattering. Tiny sparks appeared on the tops of the trees, and everything seemed to indicate that a strong storm was coming. Suddenly, in the night silence, the earth began to shake. It is not known exactly when it was, but it can be concluded that somewhere between midnight and dawn. Strong shocks and accompanying underground bangs and thumps thoroughly frightened the villagers. Terrified people ran out of their homes. At one point, those who served in the Austro-Hungarian Army thought it was an artillery cannonade. The earthquake stopped after some time, but the bang was still heard. They couldn't compare these sounds to anything, because they have never encountered anything similar. According to the description given by them, it could be compared to a constant thunder or a sound made by a big forge.

When the villagers found that no one was shooting at them and their belongings were intact, they calmed down a little. After a while, they located the direction from which these strange noises were coming from the opposite side of Magura. But because it was dark, besides waiting, they could do nothing. Then they gathered in front of the houses and waited what would happen next. A strong bang ended as suddenly as it began. From the accounts, it can be concluded that it didn't last longer than tens of seconds.

After a moment of silence, the people thought the night performance was over, but it wasn't. When they returned to their homes, they suddenly heard a strong, high squeak that penetrated them all the way to the bone. It came from all directions and it didn't help to cover the ears - they hear it all the time. This time, however, the sound was accompanied by light. From the other side of Magura, bright flashes of light flew toward the cloudy sky. It could have been ordinary lightning, but according to an oral account, the light flew from the inside of the mountain into the sky, and not the other way around. Besides that, except for the amazing squeal, you couldn't hear anything else, not even thunder.

This "light and sound" show didn't last long, only a few several seconds. The inhabitants of the village waited long afterward to see whether there would be any continuation of this, but there was only night silence interrupted by the voices of animals and birds from the nearby dense forests.

Legend has it that a strong bang and lights also awakened residents of settlements and villages on the other side of Magura. The squeak was reportedly heard even in Oravská Polhora (about 7 km from Magura as the crow flies), but it couldn't be confirmed.

On the second day, a group of men from the village went to explore the opposite slope of Magura, where the lights were seen and from where the mysterious noises were coming. Throughout the day they searched the dense forests and found nothing. Nowhere was even a trace of what was happening in that area last night.

After the setting of the sun, the villagers waited with fear for the return of mysterious phenomena. They set up guards and observation posts that had been watching Magura's peak all night. But this time there were no lights or sounds.

Three weeks passed, after which a short but strong rumble came from the same place. Some compared it to the neighing of a huge horse. In the evening, the neighbors noted the disappearance of an elderly couple living on the edge of the village by the forest wall. At home, nothing was lost, no signs of struggle or violence were found. There was still hot ashes in the stove, which meant that the old people had to leave the hut in the afternoon.

On the second day, several farm animals disappeared. It turned out that a few hens, a cow, goat, and a dog disappeared without a trace. No trace was found of what had happened to them. Over the next few days, several other animals disappeared.

Four days after the events described, one of the village shepherds was looking for a stray sheep on Magura's slope. Not too far away in the forest, he came across a "bottomless" hole in the ground. It was perfectly round, and a terrible stench was coming from it. The shepherd noticed that the branches of trees above the hole were leafless and twisted. Because he knew about the events of four days ago, he alerted the peasants of the settlement. They immediately connected a strange hole with a light-sound spectacle that had scared them in the previous days. Again they heard a strange thunder that seemed to come from the depths of the Earth. It sounded as if from a great distance. There was no doubt that something was moving down there.

From the word of mouth, it can be concluded that the hole was punched vertically in the mountain slope. It looked like a well - its internal walls were perfectly smooth. Its diameter was about 50-60 cm. Frightened but determined; the peasants threw a rope-bound stone into this well to measure its depth. After unrolling the entire rope, the stone didn't reach the bottom. Converting the depth to today's measures, the rope was 25-30 m long.

No man dared to get into this hole and find out what was hidden in it. They were discouraged by the hideous smell coming out of the well and the muffled murmurs coming out from below the ground. They limited themselves only to look around to check whether they would find traces of an animal that could have its lair in the hole. They found only a piece of linen and a cow's horn. Despite wet weather, the linen was dry, and it was obvious that it got there quite recently. It came from a shirt. The cow's horn was also short in the forest, and it was cut off from the cow's head a few days earlier.

With these modest search results, the villagers returned to the settlement. What they saw couldn't be explained in any way. No one had heard of the hole in the forest before, although some families had lived under Magura for many generations.

The earth shook that same evening. This time it was before midnight. The shocks lasted only a few seconds (according to legend, it took as long as counting to ten, and therefore 8-12 seconds), which was enough for people to run outside the huts. Thanks to this, they noticed that again on the other side of Magura a strong light was burning, whose glow lit up the night sky. Again, they heard a strong bang similar to the one that had scared them a few weeks earlier. The bang gradually turned into a high squeak and died down at once. At the same moment, also the glow disappeared.

A few days later, several bravest peasants went to this place from which light and sound came. They noticed that there was a landslide. There were several upturned trees, the slope itself changed a little, and the mysterious hole disappeared. Just disappeared. There is no trace left of it.

Here the event, or Legend, which a couple of villagers told me 40 years ago, is over. According to them, nothing happened after that. No lights or unusual noises were observed. Missing people and animals weren't found, and nobody knows what really happened to them.

Due to the long period of time, it cannot be determined whether the events described above took place really or only in the heads and imaginations of simple villagers. At first glance, it would seem that it is only about an unusual legend, which, passed by word of mouth, from father to son, has been distorted to the form quoted above. Studying literature, however, you can come across similar information from around the world on very similar events.

It seems to us that there is some explanation for the strange phenomena that have been observed around Magura. One of the elements of the solution to this puzzle is the weather and the associated movements of rock, earth and water masses - landslides. As for the Beskids, the phenomenon of landslides is known there and it is not surprising to anyone, especially during the humid summer months and the autumn floods. Even in the vicinity of Jordanów, there is a place where this phenomenon occurs very often. **Stanisław Bednarz**, MA, writes on this subject in his article entitled "Landslides around Jordanów" in "Echo Jordanowa" no. V-VI / 2000, the extensive fragments of which we will allow ourselves to quote:

In the Jordanów area, the massif of the Przykrzec mountain (741 m a.s.l.) is a highly developed landslide area. It results from the specific geological structure of this hill. Thick-bed sandstones that build the utmost parts are lined with a package of hydrated argillaceous shale. The gradual leaching of underlying argillaceous formations violates the stability of the peak sections built of sandstone. This manifests itself in numerous and sudden landslides. These processes were particularly active during rainy years. Thorough research, which I conducted in 1982-85, showed occurrence of 15 landslides. Fortunately, the slopes of Przykrzec are undeveloped and there is no threat to the facilities.

The largest landslide No. 1 covers the northern slopes of the side branch of Przykrzec - the so-called Grapy (700 m a.s.l.) - covers an area of approx. 30 ha. Currently, it's closed. It arose about 5,000 years ago in the Atlantic phase of the Holocene when the climate was extremely humid. It is one of the largest landslides in the Carpathians. By the way, it is, next to the Osielec Quarry, a perfectly visible object in satellite photos taken from Landsat -1.

Another landslide is formation No. 11 on the southern slope of Przykrzec and comes from modern times. It arose during the extremely rainy summer of 1848. This fact is remembered by many residents of Jordanów, because it was accompanied by the roar of shifting rock masses, heard even in the center of Jordanow. This landslide is known to most geologists in the country, because its photo from 1948 is in the leading textbook of university geology entitled "Geologia dynamiczna" by Prof. Marian Książkiewicz. The trace visible in the form of a non-overgrown scar in the mountain slope was visible until the mid-1970s.

We remember the emergence of a smaller landslide on Przykrzec one rainy summer in the mid-1960s. At night we were woken by a loud bang and we felt the underground shock. In the morning we saw a wide crack in the southeast slope of this mountain. Now, in 2003, this scar is no longer visible, and it is covered by a dense spruce forest, but at the time the cliff was several dozen meters high, and then it was the destination of local people and vacationers. So, we can safely assume that a landslide on the Magura slope was created as a result of underground shocks and the launching of water-saturated thousands of tons of soil and rocks that flowed down creating a massive avalanche that destroyed everything that got in its way. This is the first aspect of this matter.

It will be much more difficult to explain the strange lights and noises that have been observed in this area, but there is also a solution. Although this may sound ridiculous, it is possible that these villagers have preserved the memory of the fall of two iron meteorites to Earth: *Meteorite Lenarto* (1813) - ML and *Meteorite (Oravska) Magura* (1830-1840) – MOM". In parentheses, I give the years of their discovery, because everything indicates that they fell much earlier. (All data is from the websites: www.meteorite.fr and www.meteorites.ru). According to Slovak and Hungarian astronomers and meteorologists, (at that time Slovakia was part of the former Austro-Hungarian Monarchy, hence fragments of both meteorites were exhibited in one of the museums in Budapest), the fall of these two meteorites is surrounded by a dense fog of mystery. So far, no one has determined when they actually fell to Earth, perhaps somewhere around the turn of the eighteenth and nineteenth centuries. ML of IIIA-Om classification type fell near the village of Lenartov near Bardejov, at an approximate position 49°N - 021°E - according to astronomers, 2 km south of the Polish border - that is, more precisely at 49°18'33"N - 021°01'19"E, where the center of Lenartov is located. On the other side of the border is the

Polish village of Dubne. MOM of IA-Og classification type, fell at an approximate position 49°20'N - 019°29'E - i.e. about 4.5 km west of Tvrdošín and 2 km northwest from the village of Zemanska Dedina, also at a short distance from the Polish border - about 10-12 km as the crow flies. The main mass of this meteorite rests in the vicinity of the former village of Slanica, i.e. where the waters of the Orava Lake are buzzing today - according to the publication of Slovak astronomer **Dr. Vladimír Porubčan** on the website of *Matica Slovenska*.

There is also a third mysterious flying object that fell at noon on August 6, 1662, on the summit dome of Slavkovský štít - today measuring 2,452 m a.s.l. - in the Slovak High Tatras at 49°09'54"N - 020°11'18"E, causing an extensive stone to run on its slopes. This is how the event was described by **Dr. Jacek Kolbuszewski** in his book "Skarby króla Gregoriusa" (Katowice 1972):

The day of August 6, 1662, was long remembered by the inhabitants of northern Slovakia. On that day the earth suddenly shook - and the quake was so strong that not only the walls of the houses in Levoča, Kežmarok and Spišská Nová Ves were cracked, but even some (rich in noble liquors.) basements collapsed. However, those whose eyes were turned towards the Tatra Mountains at the time of the quake could see how the entire top of Slavkovský štít turns into rubble, the rock avalanche crushes the forests, how a large, black cloud arises over the mountains. Gifted with the greatest perceptiveness, they saw the perpetrator of the entire incident - a huge dragon flying high above the Tatra Mountains. This event was commemorated by Gaspar Hain, chronicler of the city of Levoča, a calm and sensible man, impressive with the inquisitiveness of his mind. He determined without error that the dragon chose the so-called Hochwald as its lair - the surroundings of the village of Štrba today. However - unfortunately - there are no traces of this dragon today.

(See: Kolbuszewski J. - "Skarby króla Gregoriusa," Katowice 1972; Anthology "Bolid Syberyjski," Jordanów 2002 [script]; Leśniakiewicz R. - "Projekt Tatry," Cracow 2002).

Earlier, Slavkovský štít had to measure at least 200 m more, and was equal to or even higher than Gerlach, which measures 2,655 m a.s.l. In the seventeenth century, it was still thought so. Today, you can see this rocky rubble, going to this peak along the tourist trail No. 2906 (blue signs) from Starý Smokovec. The shock after the impact was so strong that the walls of houses cracked, and basements collapsed in nearby towns. So, it must have been an earthquake measuring about 4.0 - 4.5 on the MSK scale. If you believe the written records of those times, a fragment of this cosmic body ricocheted and fell somewhere near the village of Hochwald - today's town of Štrba, located between Poprad and Liptovský Mikuláš. (The description of this event was made in Hungarian and German. During World War II, this chronicle was taken to Prague and disappeared there without news. Dr. Miloš Jesenský was looking for it in the 1990s, and hence we know that only a copy of it has survived to this day.) We offer for it the name Meteorite Vysoké Tatry - MVT. We are convinced that MVT was a stone meteorite (if it was at all - sic.), because otherwise its metal debris would be quickly found and properly used. There is an alternative explanation to the origin of this cosmic body. It was an artificial space object that was in orbit since the atomic wars of the gods-astronauts and fell from orbit into the Tatra Mountains on that fateful day of August 6, 1662.

The Orava Magura is located about 15 km southeast from the Magura Mountain in the Orava Beskids. Lenartov is more or less in the same direction – except that the distance is much greater, and it is about 100 km as birds flies. Perhaps people saw the fall of MOM first, and after a few weeks, of ML? The impact of these meteorites caused earthquakes. Maybe it was just coincidence (meteorite impacts and local earthquakes). After all, this area of the Carpathians is a penseismic area and from time to time the earth trembles here as well. In 1995, when the earth shook in the belt from Czarny Dunajec to Bukowina Tatrzańska and Jurgów. These were minor shocks - together $\leqslant$ 3°MSK, but this was enough to cause anxiety in humans and animals. Especially the latter behaved restlessly before the shocks: the dogs were barking and howling, cows were roaring, horses were neighing and kicking, and so on, and so forth ("Trzęsienie ziemi na Podhalu" in "Tygodnik Podhalański" No. 44/1995; "Ziemia zatrzęsła się w Czarnym Dunajcu" in "Nasze Strony" No. 44/1995; Leśniakiewicz R. - "Koniec świata na Podhalu?" in "TP" No. 45/1995).

So, their unusual behavior can be explained by this. The same sounds of squeaking or whistling – it could have been an electrophone meteorite, i.e. one that, when flying through the atmosphere, produces electromagnetic waves that affect the human hearing center in the brain. Such effects have been observed more than once, so this explanation also explains a lot.

When did it occur? It could have been several centuries ago. Legends passed by word of mouth, from father to son are extremely lively, and on the other hand time in such small, isolated from the world communities passes in a completely different, natural rhythm of nature's transformation, so this legend can be 200, 300, or even 500 and more years old. It seems that we are dealing with a distant echo of two (or maybe more) falls of meteorites on the Slovak-Polish borderland in the distant past. Why the certainty that it can be about meteorites? Please compare the description of what was happening around Magura with the descriptions given by witnesses of the fall of the Tunguski Meteor - or rather more adequately - of the Tunguski Cosmic Body. They are very similar, and therefore, it could have been a phenomenon similar to the TCB fall, but on a much smaller scale. The difference is that no traces of TCB were found, in contrast to ML and MOM ones. They can be admired at the museums. At the Museum of the East Slovak Country in Košice I saw several kilograms of iron fragments of both these meteorites. At the Orava regional museums, we can admire agricultural tools made of meteorite iron, originating from MOM (See: Żbik M. - "Tajemnice kamieni z nieba," Warsaw 1987; Brzostkiewicz St. R. - "Komety - ciała tajemnice," Warsaw 1985; Pilski A. S. - "Nieziemskie skarby," Warsaw 1999; Yeomans D. - "Komety," Warsaw 1999).

Meanwhile, all these strange events - described by A. Vit'azia - we associate with another topic, namely - the question arises whether they may have any connection with the Glass Wall Tunnel in Babia Góra of Dr. Eng. Jan Pająk and Dr. Antonin Horák's Moon Cave? It doesn't seem so at first glance, but...

Legends of mysterious caves are common all over the world. What we consider to be natural formations, several dozen centuries ago may have been the work of man. Once, we visited the ruins of the complex of Hitler's *Wolfsschanze* Headquarters in Gierłoż near Kętrzyn and we noticed the calcium stalactites and stalagmites formed there - sometimes colored by iron compounds in a whole range of colors - from yellow to dark brown. The same was found in the bunkers of the Pomeranian Wall fortifications, Międzyrzecz Fortification Region or the underground crypts of the Owl Mountains. Only 58 years have passed since the creation of these fortifications and their destruction, and typical karst phenomena have already appeared there. We suspect that in a hundred years there will be a regular speleothem. And what will be there in a thousand years and 10,000? Underground tunnels and shafts will be full of charming stalactites, stalagmites, stalagnates, cave pearls, milk of lime, soda straws and other karst phenomena, and only some details will suggest that they are not of natural origin. That's why we think some caves – even those in the Tatras, Pieniny, Beskids, Sudetes or Świętokrzyskie Mountains, and even in the Tri-City area – can be of artificial origin.

Another circumstance is the exploitation of natural resources in the mountains. Reviewing the work titled "Tatrzański Park Narodowy" (Cracow-Zakopane 1985) of a team of scientists from several Polish universities, we found that the Polish part of Tatra Mountains is extremely poor in minerals. The situation is similar with the Slovak part. Why? After all, in the mountains veins of various metals were found, or themselves in their native form: gold, silver, copper, antimony, iron, arsenic, and others. Here the miserable remains, not even deserving of "honest" exploitation. It's weird - isn't it? Or maybe these deposits have already been exploited, and we only have the miserable remnants and caves, which were once shafts and tunnels, and now got covered with speleothems and eroded by water and tectonic displacements. The metal and wooden supporting structures fell apart and corroded over the centuries, and today we can only admire the remains of the magnificent constructions of underground mines and processing plants, which during the Atlantean Empire operated at full capacity. Yet the remains of devices could remain in the form of inclusions in calcite, alabaster or aragonite nodules. You would have to look for them on the lowest floors of bottom cave sediments, where calcite quickly covered objects left at the bottom of the caves. Who knows, if one beautiful day we will find an artifact immersed in limestone, like the "astronomical calculator from Rhodes" or the "spark plug" from the Coso geoid. We think that this search should finally begin. Of course, I'm not counting on finding entire artifacts or even their remains, but their traces in the form of sediments of unusual metal oxides: e.g. manganese, nickel, chromium, niobium, tantalum, germanium or REE accompanying iron oxides. Something like this would be a significant clue, that we are dealing with a chemical trace of artifacts in a cave that once - 120 years ago - could have been an underground factory, a mine or even. a nuclear shelter. Admixtures of REE could be a clue to the technical advancement of this civilization, or they could indicate the reason for its fall:

nuclear war, ecological disaster, etc. Let's not forget that one of the reasons for the fall of the Atlantean Empire was the evil spells of the Black Mages, according to i.a. **Mór (Maurycy) Jókai** (1848-1904) or **W. Montyhert** in his novels (M. Jókai - "Atlantyda," Warsaw 1986, F. Montyhert - "Atlantyda i Agharta," Warsaw 1985) written under the influence of atlantological and esoteric literature at the turn of the century. (Note, as for the latter author, we suspect that it was a nickname under which hid either **Antoni Ferdynand Ossendowski** [1878-1945] or **Kamil Giżycki** [1893-1968] who could be in Siberia and came across the legend of Agartha at the same time. It could also be another well-known novelist, e.g. **Alfred Szklarski** (1912-1992), but it is rather doubtful, though not impossible). So, what dark magic? There was no black magic - there was only a sudden release of some energy that got out of the magicians' (read: scholars') control with the known effect - Chernobyl times a thousand. Or a million.

It has never been proven that such underground structures ever existed, but on the other hand, no one has ever looked for them. Because there is no one to believe in them except a handful of outsiders. Maciej Kuczyński, already cited here, claims that he was in many caves around the world and found no traces of Alien Civilizations or our predecessors. Of course - all traces fell to dust, turned into rust, oxides, hydroxides, sulfides, sulfates, sulfites, halides, etc., and it would be a miracle to find some metal artifact. Let's not forget that already dozens, maybe hundreds of years have passed, maybe even millions. When looking at museum exhibits, we rarely realize that they are tens, hundreds, or often even thousands of years old. Seeing them, we are aware of the mists of time that they come from. Still exist only the ones that have been created from the most durable material: stone or baked clay - others survived miraculously in favorable conditions, preserved in: clay, soil, peat, salt or petroleum, asphalt or earth wax. Still, others fell to dust or corroded. This was the case with all artifacts hidden in the bosom of the Earth. That's why Maciej

Kuczyński is right in saying that there was nothing there because it had no right to be.

But - there is one more thing: Maciej Kuczyński claims that the Tatras have been completely examined in terms of speleology, and that nothing new will be found there. He is wrong. In "Tygodnik Podhalański" No. 36/2003 of September 4, 2003, on p. 19 there is: "THE GREAT DISCOVERY IN ČERVENÉ VRCHY. Fakro Hall larger than the St. Mary's Basilica in Cracow." The author of this report is **Wojciech W. Wiśniewski.** "*The Little Cave in Mułowa - the largest cave discovery that has been made in Poland for over 15 years - reveals further secrets. Last year, in a small, long-known cave located in the Ciemniak massif, a great extension and the largest cave chamber in our country, later called the Fakro Hall, was discovered. The news of this extraordinary discovery spread all over Poland. In August, during the recently ended camp, cavers from Sądecki Klub Taternictwa Jaskiniowego PTTK, led by Anna Antkiewicz, made further sensational discoveries in the Little Cave. They deepened it to 400 meters and discovered the second deepest cave well in Poland.*

The Fakro Hall is a gigantic cave chamber, the ceiling of which is 90 m above the bottom of the hall, its length is 85 m and width is 40 m. The entire St. Mary's Basilica with both towers would fit there.

During further actions, we made another impressive discovery in the Little Cave. We explored a series of corridors and wells with a total length of approx. 800-850 m - as if a whole new cave. The depth reached has given the Little Cave the 5th position on the list of the deepest caves in Poland. 1.5 km of corridors and wells were explored in it, which places it on the 14th position in terms of length in Poland. In the new parts, there is a large, vertical well, 130 m deep; the second deepest in Poland," he writes.

So, as you can see, the Tatra Mountains showed us one more surprise. The Tatras have many things to discover, because their underground world is *terra nondum cognita* - a land not completely known. In 1998, the Wesoła Warszawka Hall was discovered in the Great Snowy Cave in the Červene vrchy massif. The cave itself has been known since 1959. The rock edifice of Červene vrchy is riddled with caves and many discoveries await us there. In general, Červene vrchy is a mysterious massif and strange things are happening on it, which are described in "Projekt Tatry."

The mountains are empty. To that conclusion came **Marcin Gala**, the author of the article "Góry od środka" in "Wiedza i Życie" No. 4/2004. He didn't reinvent the wheel. Scholars such as **Werner Bauer** called **Agricola** or **Anastasius Kircher** and their followers had already written about it. Contemporary scholars are "discovering" with astonishment what was already known 300 or more years ago.

This is proof that we don't know deeply the mountains, which we every day look at - what's more - we don't know the mountains which apparently have been thoroughly examined by scientists and speleologists. Will this be the case with the Moon Cave??? But let's go back *ad rem*.

The mysterious well could be therefore a cave of tectonic origin, not karst - because the Beskids massifs consist mainly of hard sandstones, and only earthquakes are able to violate their continuity so that larger rock voids are created in them. It also cannot be ruled out that it was some kind of adit or shaft - the story shows that it was rather a shaft that could run to horizontally located passages carved in the Magura massif. Perhaps some animals lived there, hence the stench of their excrements or bodies coming out from there, as suggested by Maciej Kuczyński. In addition, the Beskids are built of tertiary sandstones (Magura, Godul, and Istebna) of various colors and hardness, whose beds are even 1,600-2,000 m thick, but they lie on carbonate formations (marl, chalk, marly slates, conglomerate) and volcanic (teschenites) from Cretaceous, so under the hard sandstone "cap" there may be huge caves and rock voids. A similar situation prevails in Červene vrchy, where hard "caps" of crystalline rocks lie on carbonate deposits, and underneath there are caves with huge halls (see the Fakro Hall already mentioned in the Little Cave.) There may be whole underground worlds that we don't even know about.

There are caves in these sandstones, but they arose as a result of tectonic movements (cleft caves). That is why the Glass Walls Tunnel of prof. Pająk could actually arise in Babia Góra sandstones and led to the hypothetical karst cave system below its peak. As has been said in previous publications, legends about the underground world of the Beskids spread persistently and are passed down from generation to generation. We believe that there is also some part of the truth in them and simply people penetrating the mountains encountered traces of ancient mining of mineral deposits, which they considered manifestations of the activity of evil powers - which comes out every time when reading so-called "spiski" - these first guides to the Tatras and other mountains of the country and neighboring countries (Wojterski T. – "Babia Góra," Warsaw 1983; Krygowski Wł. – "Beskidy – Przewodnik," Warsaw 1974, vol. 1; Matuszczyk A. – "Beskid Wyspowy – Przewodnik," Pruszków 2001; Niedźwiedź A., Figiel St. – „Beskidy," Bielsko-Biała 1998, vol. 1; Nowicki W. – "Beskid Sądecki," Bielsko-Biała 2001, Krzywda P. – "Grupa Babiej Góry," Warsaw 2001).

CHAPTER 9

Fire from clouds and extraterrestrial object under the Tatra Mountains

From unknown orbital objects to strange cars - *Archive X* in the Polish style: The army is looking for a meteorite - earthquakes, and stones flying from the sky - Underground signals from Argentina - Ufocatastrophe in Slovakia?

Now we would like to share with the readers another strange event that does not have much in common with the main topic of this work but sheds some light on the problem of the existence of the Moon Cave and entire underground worlds.

We have already written about strange phenomena that took place around Cracow, (Leśniakiewicz R.: "Nieznane obiekty orbitalne" w "Nieznany Świat," nr 3(99) (1999), p.42-44, Leśniakiewicz R.: "Projekt Tatry," Kraków 2002, p.192-196), and related to the phenomenon called the *Jerzmanowice Meteorite*. The name comes from the village of Jerzmanowice, located 19 km north-west of Cracow's toll booths, at route 94 (E-40), 15 km before Olkusz. Since this event falls within the scope of interest of the Center for Research on UFOs and Anomalous Phenomena in Cracow as a Close Encounter of the Second Kind, the case was given the reference *CE2 Jerzmanowice 19930114-A* and we are constantly gathering materials in the hope that this secret will one day be clarified. Now we will briefly remind the course of events:

In the evening, on January 14, 1993, around 7 pm in Jerzmanowice something terribly flashed, there was a paralyzing bang that was heard within a radius of at least 30 km. In the village itself, televisions, telephones, radios, and other electrical appliances ceased to work, at least within 1,000 m from the epicenter of the explosion. There was no power in the power grid. No one could find the cause of this phenomenon. Moments after the explosion, people felt a disgusting smell, like "Azotox" or another strong insecticide. For the next week, people felt either overly energized or oppositely - apathetic and sleepy. Similarly, pets. And then there began to be born. triplets - as **Anna Szulc** (Gazeta Krakowska of October 1, 1994) and **Izabela Pieczara** (Gazeta Krakowska of January 28/29, 1995) reported in their newspaper stories.

The epicenter of the explosion was at the top of the hill called Babia Góra, located at 50°12'25"N and 019°45'30"E. The explosion had to be very strong and its energy broke into small pieces, several centimeters in diameter, the tip of a limestone monadnock also called Skałka 502, and the splitting of this debris formed a 200 x 700 m ellipse, from SE to NW. It was calculated on its basis that such a destructive effect would be caused by detonating 80-100 kg of 2,4,6-trinitrotoluene – have gun HTNT at the top of Babia Góra. The flash of the explosion was apparently seen even in Zawoja - a town about 70 km away from the zero point of the mysterious explosion. It is hard to believe because Zawoja was built in a quite deep valley between the Babia Góra range and the Jałowice range of the Beskids, so it is hard to suppose that this flash was seen in the thd "llage - it's more likely that from the shelters on Markowe Szczawiny and Hala Krupowa - from where there is a magnificent view up to the Świętokrzyskie Mountains on the north.

Now, the most interesting. On January 15, 1993, at 7:00 am, Babia Góra and nearby Sikorka were surrounded by a cordon of the Military Police, which allowed no local people to enter the area of explosion. Just like in some kitschy series made in Hollywood. After some time, other soldiers from the Chemical Forces from Cracow came to the place, who - according to the accounts of witnesses - were collecting and testing something with the help of metal detectors and Geiger counters. After a week or even two, the military left the area claiming that they didn't find anything and allowed astronomers and meteorologists from the Jagiellonian University and other domestic and foreign universities to enter this place. They also found nothing. The large sums offered by collectors to those who would find some meteorite shard also didn't help - nothing was found, except for small, limestone pebbles, into which the explosion turned the tip of Babia Góra's limestone inselberg.

Appear the first analyzes of the phenomenon developed by the scientists: **Dr. Jan Mietelski** in "Wiedza i Życie" No. 5,1993; **Janusz Płeszka** and **Tomasz Ścięcor** in "Postępy astronomii" No. 4,1994 and "Urania" No. 6,1993 and **Krzysztof Włodarczyk** ibid and in "Młody Technik" No. 5,1993. The hard part now begins.

It turns out that we don't know such an obvious thing which is the direction from which this strange guy from the Universe flew to Jerzmanowice. There are four versions of the arrival of *Jerzmanowice Wonder* as seen by the inhabitants of: Rudnik, Jerzmanowice, Przeginia, Cracow, Szklary, Sąspowa, Zabierzów, Brzezinka, Psar, Siedlec, Żbik, Miękinia, Pisar, Łaz, Balice, Skawina and Zawoja. - towns located 0.5 to 70 km from the epicenter. Witnesses saw the passage of a fireball, leaving a trace as if a contrail. The ball was golden-red to orange. This UAV hit the rock of Babia Góra and broke its upper part in a very strong, white-blue flash of light, thanks to which the energy of this explosion was estimated – it was 100 MJ.

Here's the second puzzle - an explosion of this power should have caused a local earthquake. The seismic station of the Institute of Geophysics of the Polish Academy of Sciences in Ojców, 3 km away from the zero point, recorded the first shock at

6:58:54 pm, and at 7:00:17 pm the second seismic shock coming from the direction of Jerzmanowice, with their characteristics indicating that Babia Góra was hit by two lightning bolts. It is true that on this day and at this hour a cold atmospheric front was moving above this area, accompanied by storm clouds from which the discharges were coming. All right, in that case, where is the shock from the explosion of *Jerzmanowice Wonder*???

The third secret – after the explosion that broke the tip of Babia Góra limestone inselberg (on the shards), there wasn't found the impact of high temperature, and it should have been there. At least because the white-blue flash of the explosion indicates the impact of temperatures of ≥100.000 K. This is thermonuclear fusion temperature. There were found "lightning signs" on Babia Góra, but again, where is the meteorite that must have hit Babia Góra? Because otherwise, it would probably have formed an astrobleme or after-impact crater in the event of a soil hit.

The fourth secret: what caused the failure of the electrical network and all receivers connected to it? The explanation was found – it was an electrophone meteorite. And here a word of explanation. These are the meteorites that fly through the atmosphere creating various audiovisual effects, thanks to the fact that their passage produces a cool plasma – highly ionized gas – which in turn is a source of electromagnetic waves causing the effect of MP - magnetic pulse and various audible sounds (actually perceived as acoustic effects) not through the ears, but through the human brain. The following table shows the coinciding points of the fall of electrophone meteorites with the fall of *Jerzmanowice Wonder*:

Date	Place	Audio and visual effects
12.01.1706	Tobolsk (RUS)	Passage of the fireball (UAV) and grinding noise

08.1898	Finland	Passage of the UAV and the sound of a paper tearing
01.23.1913	Ochotnica Górna (PL)	Passage of the UAV and the sound of thunder
04.1928	Laredo (USA)	Passage of the UAV and a moaning sound
03.01.1929	Chmielowka (RUS)	flash of light and rustling ended with thunder
08.10.1937	Omsk (RUS)	flash of light and loud noise
05.1944	Ashgabat (TKM)	Passage of the UAV, whistling and crackling
10.04.1950	Missouri (USA)	Passage of the UAV, whistling and moaning - heard only by children.
04.07.1978	Sydney (AUS)	Passage of the UAV, whistling and crackling
1982	Isikule (RUS)	Passage of the UAV, the sound of a canvas tearing
01.14.1993	Jerzmanowice (PL)	Passage of the UAV, bang and whistle
12.09.1993	New Zealand	Passage of the UAV, the whistle ended with a bang
06.30.2001	Skomielna Biała	Loud whistle and bang

Professor L. P. Drawert calculated that by 1950, 267 electrophone meteorites had fallen to Earth. Jerzmanowice Wonder also fits into this pattern. It was assumed, therefore, that first the meteor fell, which went out just above the Earth's surface, and immediately afterwards there were two lightning strikes that used the ionized air channel, and which caused the explosion – actually the electro-explosion of the rainwater accumulated in the crevices of a limestone rock. This is what the "scientists" explained.

As for the Skomielna Biała Meteorite, it could have been a piece of cosmic ice that fell to Earth in the forest surrounding Luboń Wielki from the village of Skomielna Biała and melted there, and the whistle was just the sound of the air torn by it, but we are not sure about it.

But what could the Jerzmanowice meteorite be? It exactly meets the definition of an Unidentified Flying Object (UFO.) To this day, we don't know exactly what it was. Just like in the case of the Tunguski Meteorite, we fall into the trap of terminology. This thing underwent a total disintegration during the explosion. It was the air explosion, because in the case of a ground explosion, the earth would shake, and it would be immediately recorded in Ojców. But it could have been so, which no one took into account, that the first shock - the one at 6:58:54 PM - was a shock caused by the explosion of *Jerzmanowice Wonder*, while the second one - at 7:00:17 PM was its "seismic echo" reflected from something that was under the epicenter of the explosion. Perhaps this thing is a large and empty space, located under Ojców National Park, a cavern or a cave.

Another point - the *thing* that exploded there must have been of artificial origin, because no typical meteorite matter was found at the site of the impact, and instead, aluminum balls of clearly artificial origin were found, as shown by tests using scanning and electron microscopes, thanks to which the EDS spectrum of the tested samples was obtained. SEM-EDS spectra showed a large amount of aluminum - Al, and slightly less iron (Fe) in two samples, in the total absence of other elements, while another sample contains: silicon (Si), aluminum (Al), calcium – (Ca), potassium, K and higher iron content than in the other two samples. Scientists considered the third sample to be typically Earthly due to potassium, calcium and silicon contamination, while the other two were typically extraterrestrial - perhaps from a meteorite. The authors say that perhaps it was a fragment of the 6344 P-L asteroids from the Apollo group, which "got lost" a few years ago. The astronomers' calculations show that the asteroid 6344 P-L on January 14 and 30, 1993, almost grazed the Earth's atmosphere.

If so, the composition of Jerzmanowice Wonder was extremely interesting: almost chemically pure aluminum with an admixture of iron. After all, it fits into an artificial satellite of the Earth, not a meteorite. Or maybe it was that the asteroid 6344 P-L threw into the Earth's atmosphere some artificial satellite that fell just near Jerzmanowice. Note, something similar could have happened on April 15, 1995, near Węgorzewo, where some Unidentified Flying Object fell, which was later taken by boys from GROM and several sad men from Warsaw in an unknown direction – as **Bronisław Rzepecki** once wrote about in "Czas UFO." It could have been a secret, military, artificial satellite of the Earth. And even earlier, because on January 21, 1959, some Soviet or American SSZ fell into port basin No. IV in Gdynia, hence the rumor about a UFO crash on the coast. The events that took place in the late 40s near Ustka, I described in the "Nieznany Świat" in 2002. Who said a flying saucer crashed there? Maybe already then, the Soviet space apparatus flew over the Polish coast and was evacuated to the Soviet army base in Bornem-Sulinów, and then to the USSR. In all cases, acted the army, which exported artifacts in an unknown direction - I suspect that to Moscow, and after 1989 - to Washington. There also could have been sent the collected debris of the satellite that fell on Jerzmanowice.

There is also the other side of the coin, about which I wrote to the quarterly of Polish Meteorite Society "Meteoryt." Let me quote the lion's share of this article because it also provides some explanation for this case:

[...] Currently, we don't even know what it really was. Meteorite? - then why its remains are not there? - the army picked them up, but for what? Lightning strikes? - it is doubtful that two lightnings struck the same place in a short interval of time and produced such an effect. Electricity flows down the surface of the rock to the ground and does not immediately penetrate the rock and causes water to evaporate, or even to dissociate it into hydrogen and oxygen, which could have caused an explosion due to the formation of a fulminating mixture. Finally, the disaster of the spy plane, the explosion of the bomb, the missile or artillery – this is the most reliable explanation and justifies the presence of the Military Gendarmerie and military specialists who, for known reasons, took the remains of this "thing" so that they didn't fall into the wrong hands.

However, there is one more possibility that is only beginning to be discussed in the world, and it is related to the ongoing war on terrorism. Specifically, the terrorist attack on the Indonesian island of Bali, the responsibility for which was officially claimed by the al-Quaeda organization on its website. The thing, however, is not how the coup was organized, but with the help of what. Officially, there were about several hundred kilograms of 2,4,6-trinitrotoluene - or TNT, which were detonated in the vicinity of entertainment venues with a known effect: several hundred dead and wounded, huge material losses, panic and shock. But was that a TNT? Police and military specialists have more and more doubts because the amount of TNT that should have been used to achieve such a destructive effect would have to be transported by truck -

meanwhile, living witnesses in unison agree that no truck was seen there. So, what remains?

In the early 1990s, Polish special services were alarmed by information coming from the CIS, saying that from the weapon warehouses of the former Soviet Army disappeared in unexplained circumstances and without a trace about 100 miniature nuclear devices of low power. These heads had the form of a suitcase (hence the name - "suitcase bombs") with approximate dimensions of 75 x 60 x 30 cm, weight 30 - 50 kg, made of aluminum. Their power ranged from 0.0001 - 1 kt of TNT, i.e. from 100 kg to 1,000 tons of trotyl. The worst thing about it is that after the explosion of such a charge there is practically no radioactive fall-out, while the residues emit β *and* γ *radiation in quantities that lie within the measurement error and thus are almost undetectable for normally used radiometers, and* α *radiation disappears quickly - it is not so dangerous anyway, because even a piece of paper stops it. The working factor in these bombs is a small amount of plutonium-239 stabilized with plutonium-240 and submerged in the reflector which is also a source of neutrons - known as "red mercury" - RM-20/20. It is not mercury, but dimercury diantimonate hexoxide or heptoxide Hg2Sb2O6 or Hg2Sb2O7. The whole was a size of a tennis ball. The red color of this highly radioactive chemical compound (because mercury or antimony radioisotopes are used to make it) is its hallmark. I don't know if it's possible, but I remember how in the early 90s all operational, operational and control as well as line services of the Border Guard and Customs Offices at all border crossings in Poland, were sensitized to possible smuggling of this compound and other components that could be used to build a nuclear or thermonuclear bomb, from the CIS countries to the European Union and then to Libya, Iran, Iraq, the PRC, North Korea, Cuba or other countries with unstable or hostile political systems, such as Yugoslavia. Also,*

WSI and UOP (now ABW) conducted independent proceedings in this case.

Note, during these activities it was revealed that Soviet/Russian atomists were meeting with Miloševic's Yugoslavs and Saddam's emissaries, among others in Poland, Slovakia and other Central European countries. That's why sappers and specialists in weapons of mass destruction went to Kosovo in the first wave. It was expected that some of the 'mothers' stolen from the Russians would be in the arsenals of Kosovo Albanians and Serbs.

How does this relate to the case of the Jerzmanowice Meteorite? Well, as a matter of fact, no one saw the fall of this meteorite, all witnesses saw the flash first, then they heard a terrible bang, from which the windows broke and the eardrums cracked, and at the same time within a kilometer from the zero point, all electrical devices burned, regardless whether they were connected to the network or not. The explosion scattered the remains of the top of Babia Góra over a distance of 200 - 700 m around - larger stones pierced the roofs and smashed, less resistant annexes.

As you can see, the effects of the Jerzmanowice explosion resemble nuclear micro-explosion quite accurately. There is a magnetic pulse effect (MPE) that destroys all electrical circuits, there is a strange, suffocating smell of some substance that irritates the respiratory tract after an explosion, a feeling of weakness or stimulation of nervous activity that subsided after a week. And no neutron flash and radioactive fall-out flash, and instead of it, aluminum microparticles found in the soil near Babia Skała.

Is this an explanation? Looking at the whole case from the point of view of the former BPT reserve officer and retired SG officer, I think it is. I believe that this is a problem not for meteorite experts and astronomers, but for nuclear physicists and relevant intelligence and anti-terrorism services of Poland and NATO. The course of events suggests that it was simply an accident - one of the stolen "mothers" ceased to be stable and began to radiate, threatening to explode. The thieves left it in the first town they had come to – bad luck it was Jerzmanowice – and they escaped. Who were these thieves? We can only assume. Maybe they were general Jochar Dudayev's Chechens fighting for freedom, or Usama ben-Laden's al-Quaeda terrorists, or simply Russian mafia smugglers - now we can only guess. It would be a pity if the above supposition turned out to be true, because instead of a cosmic secret we would only deal with a struggle for power and domination on one side, or the murky business of the Russian mafia in Poland on the other. In no case is this good.

It's a shame - isn't it?

However, this is only a conjecture, and the truth - as always - lies in the armored safes of the Ministry of National Defense and Ministry of Interior and Administration. Or was it just a UFO catastrophe? After all, the Krakow-Balice airport service saw a flight of a luminous object towards Jerzmanowice at 18:45, and therefore, about 5 minutes before the impact. That UAV was flying under the base of clouds, i.e. at an altitude of 1,400 m a.s.l. Maybe it was a classic UFO that had a crash 19 km away? It could also be a remnant after the atomic wars of the gods that revolved around the Earth for 12,000 years and now fell, knocked off the orbit by the asteroid 6344 P-L passing close by. Why not? Since such an object as the quasi-asteroid J002E3 discovered last year, which is probably nothing more than the third stage of the **Saturn** V rocket of the **Apollo** 12 ship, which is now an artificial asteroid and has been circulating the Earth in a complicated orbit for 33 years, has remained so long, why can't the remains of the atomic wars of the gods-astronauts persist? If, for example, a radar station stood on Babia Góra, it would be not as much destroyed as completely blinded by the explosion of such a projectile.

Finally, it could be a meteorite from the following swarms:

Swarm	Activity date	Maximum activity	RA (h,m,s)	DEC (°)
δ-Cancerids	01.13-21	01.16	8 24 00	+20
Comaberenid s	11.12-01.23	01.14	11 39 59	+25
α-Lynxids	January	01.17	8 40 00	+43

But everything indicates that it couldn't be any "normal" meteorite.

We were there on April 11, 1999. We talked to witnesses, but it didn't bring much new to what we knew before. The good part of this trip was that based on the materials we collected, TVN made a two-episode program from the series "Nie do wiary," devoted to this incident. Here's what we've added to the collection of facts related to this event:

- Shortly before the explosion on Babia Góra some jet plane flew over it at a low altitude, below 50 m;
- Shortly after the explosion, the witnesses felt the strong smell of burning stone or a strong insecticide. This stench lasted 24 hours, then eased;
- Immediately after the explosion, people and farm animals felt bad. All negative symptoms disappeared after about a week;
- On the brick walls of the houses appeared spots caused by burning of the brick by high temperature – at least 1,000 K UUU, which forced the hosts to plaster again the walls facing the epicenter of the explosion. The bricks were burnt in groups of 2-3, which gave the impression that the buildings were spotted;
- During World War II, a German defense line ran through Jerzmanowice. On Babia Góra there was a large cannon firing point, which shot towards Krzeszowice.

Perhaps on Babia Góra its ammunition park has survived, which Soviet sappers didn't locate and neutralize.

- At the foot of Babia Góra, a horseshoe regrowth of bright green grass was found - exactly the same as **Bronisław Rzepecki** and **Marian Książek** found on the site of the famous CE2 in Olsztyn near Częstochowa in November 1997. We penetrated the surrounding rocks, but the green horseshoe was only below Babia Góra.

The case is still open. At the moment, the state of our knowledge on this subject allows us to stick to the military hypothesis - i.e. that 10 years ago either the Soviet, American, European or Chinese military SSZ fell there, which was then taken by the military and transported - where necessary or, relic of atomic wars of gods-astronauts from 12,000 years ago, with they dealt as above. Alternatively, it could be some "cosmic scrap:" a no longer active SSZ, the rocket booster like the object designated J002E3, or something like that. Finally, it could have been some extra-secret missile or warhead tested or lost by the Polish army and quietly taken from there to the warehouse in Cracow or to the laboratory there. And this - as we think - is the truth about the Jerzmanowice Meteorite (Leśniakiewicz R. - "Jerzmanowice 1993: ostaniec w ogniu i pytania bez odpowiedzi" in "Nieznany Świat" No. 10/2003; Leśniakiewicz R. - "Jurajskie Bliskie Spotkania z UFO" in "Nieznany Świat" No. 10/1998; Leśniakiewicz R.- "Nieznane obiekty orbitalne" in "Nieznany Świat" No. 3/1999; television show entitled "Incydent Jerzmanowicki" from the "Nie do wiary" series, TVN, 1998 part 1 and 2).

We thought we wouldn't explain this puzzling case when, on April 14, 2003, Robert came across the April edition of "Wiedza i życie," in which he found a short note written by someone signing as MM, entitled "Humanitarian Bombs."

In this note, MM describes the action of graphite bombs that were used during operations in Kosovo and Yugoslavia, as well as the so-called bomb E:

The second "humanitarian" weapon is the so-called E bomb, a device emitting a short-lasting electric pulse of enormous power. It completely destroys all electronic systems. The latest E bomb transforms the energy of an explosion of two kilograms of TNT into microwaves, burning all electronics within a kilometer.

In this context, all the strange and mysterious circumstances of this event become understandable at once: burned electronics, the presence of the army and gendarmerie, and a gag imposed on the media – just some plane lost the E bomb – a prototype with an explosive charge of 80-100 kg of TNT, which exploding, destroyed electrical and electronic devices within a radius of 1 km from the epicenter - Babia Góra in Jerzmanowice. Let's not forget that it was 1993 and military technology has advanced since then.

What does it mean? This means that the Polish army had such weapons already in 1993, and thus six years before joining NATO. This possibility was suggested by Polish specialists from the "Report" already in 1999.

Well, it's a shame that there is such an explanation, and therefore not aliens, not mysterious meteorites from outside our world, but the ordinary NLW – Non-Lethal Weapon – a weapon that doesn't kill, which got out of the army's control.

What does all this have to do with the Moon Cave and other underground worlds? Well, it has - because it seems to me that this strange event revealed a completely new view of the Krakow-Wieluń Upland. Notice, the reader that the seismographs in Ojców recorded two earth tremors, while all witnesses talk about one impact. Well, it seemed incompatible, but fortunately, there was some possibility of resolving this discrepancy in facts - and everyone is right. Why? - because the witnesses saw one explosion on *Skałka 502*, while scholars recorded with the help of seismographs that explosion at 6:58:54 PM, and a few moments later - at 7:00:17 PM the seismographs recorded the shockwave of the explosion, which returned reflected from some object located near Jerzmanowice. The time interval between these two shocks is 83 seconds, i.e. this unknown *thing* must have been at a depth of 41.5 seconds of seismic waves run from the epicenter. Seismic waves propagate at speed from 3.3 to 4.5 km/s, so it can easily be calculated that the alleged object from which the seismic waves of the Jerzmanowice explosion reflected was located at a depth of 136.95 - 186.75 km below ground level. The theory shows that this is much more than the thickness of the lithospheric plate – man average of 100 km in the continental area, and therefore something else could be responsible for this phenomenon, or we are dealing with a phenomenon whose nature we don't yet know.

Already in the 1960s, British scholars suspected that underground, in the asthenosphere, there might be some empty spaces filled not with lava, but with gases under pressure. This hypothesis was presented in **Arthur C. Clarke**'s short story "The Fires Within 1947" (In the Polish edition included in the s-f almanac "Kroki w nieznane," vol. 5, Warsaw 1974), in which the author even assumes the existence of a rational Scientific-Technical Civilization there. Sounds fantastic? - and what do we actually know about the interior of our planet? Personally, I think that the case with the Jerzmanowice explosion is even different, and that this hypothetical cave lies up to 10 km deep below the surface of the earth. Perhaps it can be reached from the Upland – here speleology hasn't yet said the last word. Perhaps it is some volcanic formation – let's not forget that 200-220 milion years ago it was an area of strong volcanism, after which the eruptive rocks remained in the southern parts of the Krakow-Wieluń Upland, and in the place of today's Krzeszowice there was a volcanic caldera with a diameter of 25 km.

In the August issue of the British "UFO Magazine" from 2003 there is an interesting note, which I quote in full:

WEIRD RADIO SIGNALS FROM UNDERGROUND PICKED UP IN ARGENTINA

Two scientists working for Fundación Instituto Cosmobiofísico de Investigaciones - FICI in Argentina, said they had detected unnatural levels of radioactivity, microwaves, electricity levels, and vibrations from inside the Earth. Omar Hesse and Jorge Millstein were measuring in the mountains near Cachi, Argentina, in June this year. They came to the conclusion that these signals - because they considered them signals, are not of natural origin, but rather come from some machinery working very deep underground.

"Vibrations clearly indicate that many kilometers below the ground level electric waves are generated, which means there is an electricity source there – and that means that some machines are working there," says Hesse.

This area was not chosen accidentally, just like that. This selection was based on four films made there by the local highlander Antonio Zuleta in 2002. They all show strange, fast-moving lights that seem to fall into the ground in the same place.

"We must return to this place with more sensitive and precise equipment," Millstein said. "This is one of the hottest places on the planet in terms of extraterrestrial activity. It is a mountain range stretching from La Poma to Cayafate."

Two researchers believe that these signals are not of this world.

"For us, the possibility that foreign ships penetrate the Earth is nothing new here in the Andes. This has been shown in many cave drawings and bas-reliefs."

What about in Central Europe? No one has yet done similar measurements, and yet such research could bring interesting results in the Polish and Slovak Tatras, as was the case with finding a mysterious object in the area of the village of Vikartovce, where the flood caused by the outflow of a small river brought on the creation of a three meters deep tielke, at the bottom of which lay a mysterious object that wasn't in any classification of things created by the forces of Nature.

The village of Vikartovce in the Low Tatras with 1,600 souls, lies at the intersection of geographical coordinates: 48°56'N - 020°10'E, in a charming valley overlooking the massif of Kráľova hoľa and Kozí chrbát, which obstructs the view of the High Tatras from the north. The find is located 2 km west, in the direction of the sources of Hornád. The workers who built the artificial hydro-technical facility discovered it when a regular ellipsoidal object protruding from the rock wall was found in its deepest place. Its top layer clearly stood out from the surrounding rock. Also, its density and cohesion was exactly different from the rock layers in which it lay. It looked like armor exposed to high temperatures.

After the discoverers, a search team from Košice led by **Dr. Martin Schuster** appeared, equipped with shovels, an excavator, a mini-lab and a G-M counter. They took samples from the armor of the object, it's interior and the surrounding rock. With the help of an excavator, they dug up part of the object, but stopped, due to the threat of landslides of thousands of tons of soil and rocks. They also failed to get below the object due to the rapid stream. Not much more was done by the group of **Dr. L'udomír Valenčík**, who dug into the underside of the object, but this caused the slope to slide:

"The mystery at the place of its occurrence is even more mysterious," says Dr. Valenčík, "-complex stratification, traces of high temperatures, geophysical anomalies. We managed to partially dig up the main object. Its sizes are impressive. We were able to examine a 10-meter, multi-layered formation resembling the shield of the giant Cyclops."

"We could conclude on the spot," says Dr. Schuster "that the water washes out an erosive gorge 0.5-3 m deep and 3-5 m wide, and at the bottom, there is this strange object, strongly trapped in the sandstone ground. The water probably destroyed the end of this strange body so that in the end we found only ferrous minerals, perhaps of natural origin, which also looked like a very old iron structure. This object was once empty because it was filled with soil exactly the same as the surrounding ground. The "armor" of the object was 2 cm thick, its exterior was perfectly smooth, black, with visible traces of layering. In places, there were visible holes resembling small volcanic craters, caused by the influence of high temperature from outside. The underside of the "armor" was perforated and strongly fused with the parent rock. The measured part - 2.6 m below the surface - was 3 m wide and 1 m high."

(See M. Schuster - 'Zahádný objekt v zemi pod Tatrami' in 'Fantastická Fakta' No. 9/2000, p. 10)

Chemical analysis of the material from the inside of the facility showed relatively high concentrations of heavy metal salts compared to samples from the surrounding soil and rocks. This applies especially to the content of such elements as: iron (Fe), manganese (Mn), lead (P), cobalt (Co), nickel (Ni,), chromium (Cr) and titanium (Ti). The amount of element discovered is in the range of 1-5%.

It is interesting that in the case of the Vikartovce find there is a positive correlation between it and the presence of radioactive minerals. Recently declassified materials indicate that geological research was conducted around the area of Kozí chrbát, which led to the discovery a few hundred meters from the find, of fairly rich deposits of lead and uranium ore from the Permian period (i.e. 220-270 MA ago), which were unusually connected with coal seams. Here the interesting thing, the G-M counter of the Košice expedition showed no signs of increased radioactivity.

"By no means, our analyzes show the presence of uranium," says Dr. Schuster. 40 other elements were found there - their content in the samples was 0.001% - but uranium wasn't there. And it was the place where it was intended to be exploited. Let's not forget that this is the middle of nowhere, where cats walk on the tables, dogs bark and fog chokes cows.

What is this object - and two other accompanying it, what is the blue "crust of bread" and what are the white balls found near this artifact - so far it is not known, not to mention the mysterious plasticine-like, dark green substance – is it dry Small Green Men??? If it was a heat shield, then the object it protected is below - in the sandstone rock and is flooded with subcutaneous waters.

Or maybe a meteorite? Maybe a lava tongue creating an intrusion in the form of a dike or sill? But how to explain the formation of a rock void? Maybe it's a huge geode? - but then why are there no quartz crystals formed in it? Space artifact?

Let's not forget that this is where the Moon Cave was first localized. It seems, however, that we will wait a long time for the solution to this puzzle.

CHAPTER 10

In the Chasms of Time

Lost generations: Is it myth or truth? We compile an overview of unwanted artifacts - Serious dating problems. Presumptions, criticisms, and comments - Human traces in tertiary limestone.

We haven't reached the Moon Cave so far, but we think it's only a matter of time. If this cave, and all other mysterious objects and places listed here, really exist, then it will be possible to reach them sooner or later.

What is the Moon Cave? This is most likely a remnant of the Platonic civilization that was here before us, and not necessarily only of it because there could be more such civilizations.

The theory of the multiplicity of previous civilizations is justified by the fact that mysterious artifacts and other traces from a distant past are found, in which, as far as scientists' research is believed, the *Homo sapiens* species couldn't exist yet. It could have been a hypothetical Dinosauroids' civilization from 65 Ma ago. It might have been a civilization - actually Interterran Supercivilization, or People of the First Generation from - staggering - 2 Ga (Giga-annums - billion years) ago, which hides from us in another dimension of Reality or below the surface of our planet - in the area of the so-called "Mohorovičić's discontinuity." (*Mohorovičić's discontinuity* or *the Moho* is the boundary between the earth's crust and the peridotite layer (the surface of the Earth's mantle), which reaches 5-10 km under the ocean floor, 30 km under the continents and up to 80 km under the recently elevated mountains. The thickness of the perodite layer is on average 50-80 km. It is characterized by a diametrically different from the normal course of seismic waves.

One of the American writers **Robin Cook** in his best-selling novel "Abduction" (New York, 2000) postulates its existence. He has interesting arguments, namely, ambiguities and gaps in the history of the development of life on Earth.

To understand this, you should go back ab ovo to the beginnings of Precambrian Archaic - about 2.7 Ga ago. Then, in the Earth's oceans, the first fruits of life begin to form, the most primitive unicellular cells that develop into the most primitive marine organisms in the Proterozoic. It took 2.1 Ga. Exactly 2,100,000,000 years – an incredible time gap. What was happening at that time? Anything could happen, including the rise of the Interferant civilization. Let's not forget that our civilizations are the aftermath of the evolutionary process that began only 600 Ma ago, during the so-called Cambrian explosion of life. That life cycle may have been swept away by a nearby Supernova explosion that occurred at a distance of, for example, 30 light-years from Earth. After the powerful radial blizzard, there were left on Earth, only bacteria and Interterrans concealed under a 15-20 kilometer layer of soil and rocks, where murderous radiation couldn't reach them. Then the evolution started for the second time and we - the People of the 2nd Generation are its fetus. That's all from Robin Cook. Lennart Lidfors made similar views in his novel "Gwiezdne przesłania" (Polish edition - Warsaw 2000), which we recommend, and in which he describes the civilizations of Atlantis and the older Atlantica. (**Dr. Lennart Lidfors** is a scientist who works at the Stockholm Svenska Atom research institute. He is an electronics engineer and also has a Ph.D. in psychology. He is currently working on crystals and energy processing. He is the author of many scientific dissertations [According to Kamila Knochenhauer]) - but in L. Linfors' works, the time horizon has tens of thousands of years. **James Redfield** also describes this in his trilogy about Shambhala. (James Redfield - "The Celestine Prophecy" [New York 1993], "The Tenth Insight: Holding the Vision" [New York 1996] and "The Secret of Shambhala: In Search of the Eleventh Insight" [New York 1999]). Of course, someone will say that this is pure section fiction having nothing to do with reality.

Hmmm, but then, how would he explain the presence of such strange artifacts, such as traces of bare and shod human feet found in rock layers from Cambrian (600-490 Ma ago) or Silurian Period (430-400 Ma ago)? No one could explain it, so breakneck hypotheses were made, which caused additional confusion. Or such a matter of the existence of a mysterious creature called *Chirotherium* (*Hiroterium*) or an animal (???) with hands. This creature left its footprints in the Triassic layers (i.e. 220-180 Ma ago) and to this day no bones of this thing exists or maybe even someone has been found? The matter is perfectly explained by the presence of People of the *First Generation* on Earth. The table below reminds us that archeological knowledge has something to be desired and so far, has not answered a number of fundamental questions:

Age (in millions of years)	Place and year of finding the artifact	Description of the artifact
0.2-0.4	Lawn Ridge (IL, USA) 1870	Metal "coin," stone "pipes" and ceramics. It should be added that the layers in which these artifacts were found are 50,000 to 410 Ma old.

0.5	The Jordan Valley (ISR) 1989	25 x 12 cm wooden plank.
1	Corfu (GR), ?	Petrified shoeprints
2	Nampa (IA, USA), 1889	Clay figurine of a man
3.6-3.8	Laetoli (TZ), 1978	Petrified human footprints
5	St. Andreas (CA, USA) 1891	Stone mortars and pestles
9	Mt. Table (CA, USA) 1869	Stone pestle
10	Baccinello (IT), 1958	Skeletons of anthropoid apes - approx. 30.
23	26 mines in California 1891	Stone mortars and pestles, and other unspecified artifacts.
30	California (USA) 1952	Fragments of the iron chain embedded in rock - the artifact was lost in unexplained circumstances.
33-55	California (USA) 1851	A nail in a lump of gold-bearing quartz.
38-55	Mt. Table (CA, USA), 1853-58, 1877	Spear points, jugs with handles, stone mortars, human remains, beads, stone axes.

40-45	Laon (FRA), 1862	A cretaceous sphere with a diameter of 6 cm and a weight of 310 g, found in a lignite deposit.
50?	Aix-en-provence (FRA), 1786-88	Coins, hammer handles and wooden tool fragments as well as a stone processing board. The account appeared in 1820.
50-55?	Philadelphia (PA, USA), 1830	A marble block with engraved letters.
55	Vöcklabruck (AUT), 1885	"Gurtl's Cube" with dimensions of 6.6 x 6.6 x 4.5 cm - the artifact was lost in unexplained circumstances.
55	Martin (SK), 1920	Fossilized human footprints in limestone.
65	Saint-Jean de Livet (FRA) 1968	Metallic polyhedral pipes found in Cretaceous deposits of chalk.
111	Glen Rose (TX, USA), 1969	14 human footprints 29.5 cm long in limestone rocks next to 134 dinosaur footprints.
150	Turkmenistan, 1983	Footprints similar to human feet in the rock.

248	Nevada (USA), 1922	Boot prints - the artifact disappeared in unexplained circumstances.
250	Kentucky, Pennsylvania, Missouri (USA), 1938	Fossilized human footprints with dimensions of 25 x 15 cm.
260-320	Morrisonville (IL, USA), 1891	An 8ct gold chain with a length of 25 cm - the artifact was lost in unexplained circumstances.
286	Macoupin (IL, USA), 1862	Human bones found in a hard coal seam - disappeared in unknown circumstances.
286	Heavener (OK, USA), 1928	6 concrete blocks in a carbon wall.
312	Wilburton (OK, USA), 1948	A metal mug found in a lump of hard coal. The artifact was lost in unexplained circumstances. In addition, another account says about a barrel-shaped silver block with traces of staves.
360	Rutherford (GB), 1844	Golden thread in a block of quartzite.
360	Lehigh (IO, USA), 1897	Stone covered with reliefs measuring 60 x 30 x 10 cm.

387	Kingoodie (GB), 1844	A nail 2.5 cm long.
509-590	Antelope Spring (UT, USA), 1968	A boot print with a dimension of 25 x 8 cm.
600	Dorchester (MA, USA) 1852	A metal vase with a dimension of 11 x 16.5 x 5 cm and wall thickness of 5 mm, made of zinc and silver alloy – today called the Roxbury conglomerate.
2,000	The Owl Mountains (PL), 1944-45	A system of corridors, adits and shafts, carved in the rocks. It was on their basis that the Nazis built some objects of the underground hall system of the "Der Riese" complex.

(Prepared on the basis of: **Michael Cremo** - "Forbidden archeology," Warsaw 2000)

It is interesting in this statement that many of these artifacts have disappeared in circumstances that have not been explained until today. Who cares for them to disappear? Certainly, some churches and religious systems, and more orthodox scholars, to whom very thought of the existence of multidimensional worlds, the Bermuda Triangle, Nessie, and UFO causes a heart attack.

But only? Perhaps the *People of the First Generation* want to stay in the shadows and the truth about their existence has not leaked to the public? So, who knows whether UFO vehicles are de facto time-planes on which *Interterrans* travel in space-time as we do in the three-dimensional space of our *continuum*? If that is the case, then the *Generation I people* could control a big piece of the

Galaxy. Let's not forget that if someone can travel in a time dimension, then space for him is no longer an obstacle. Speaking figuratively, he can travel from one end of the universe to the other in T = 0 or T » 0, which practically is the same thing. Hence, all these anomalies that are listed in the table. Thus, time is the key to solve the puzzles related to the observed anomalous phenomena.

We believe that the image would be incomplete if we illuminated it only on one side - from enthusiasts of the unknown and researchers of UFO and other anomalous phenomena on our planet, and even outside it. Therefore, on July 13, 2003, we spread the word and sought the opinion of all our friends and colleagues related to CBUFOiZA, what they think about the above material. We especially asked for critical statements, because they are tips, and valuable ones, for moves in our further research activities. The responses to our appeal are listed below in the order in which they arrived in our mailbox.

The matter became immediately interesting, because almost immediately the Cracow dowser answered - **Tomasz Stefan Gregorczyk,** MA who sent us the following story about mysterious holes in the Pieniny and Beskids. Here is his account:

I printed the last text - you deal with a lot of topics, that's true. But first things first. In July 1963, I was at the scout camp in Niedzica (I was 13). I remember perfectly training (getting a badge – I have a brown MOSO – in the watchtower in Kacwin, and then "a quick return to the camp before the storm [about 1.5 hours on foot]) and that what happened then (I probably went through the first "popularity" at that time) - and the lightning struck strongly, but there wasn't much rain. At the end of the camp, we had a night march from Niedzica-village to the Castle. Everyone was warned to, about 200-300 meters in front of the castle (the route led along a traverse of the slope above the Niedzica-Czorsztyn road from the opposite side to the Niedziczanka river) – watch out for a very deep hole in the ground secured only by a wooden trestle. The night march consisted of passing subsequent "tests" such as sewing a button, chopping wood, dressing, etc. "typically scout" skills. In total, there were seven of them, and they were deployed on the above-mentioned traverse, leading then mainly through the forest; from time to time there were clearings, but in the "hole" area we were directed down towards the castle, where the endpoint and time measurement were. I told Iza about it and this Sunday we went to Niedzica and Kacwin.

Hmmm, the area with "that" hole (I loyally admit that I wasn't above it, but it was said that it wasn't a well and there was no water at its bottom) is now behind the fence (it's been 40 years, the dam was built, "that road" disappeared) and certainly buried or concreted. The bearings didn't give much. Then we went to Kacwin. The watchtower still exists (though already in a state of destruction), the church built in 1400 by the Berzeviczy family (a spitting image of that in Rabcice south of Babia Góra) is newly plastered. As in this in Rabcice we traced the descent to the underground behind the altar. Then, on the route towards Frankowa Góra (the border passes through it), we found an underground tunnel about 11 steps wide (just over 10 m). Somewhere in the slope of Frankowa Góra, a buried (or otherwise isolated) entrance to the tunnel. But this tunnel is not a main one, it is a side branch. Pictures showed a lot of pink energy, and in the church in Kacwin, a lot of white energy.

Tomasz Stanisław Gregorczyk
Cracow, July 21, 2003

It is a great pity that Mr. Tomasz Gregorczyk didn't take any closer interest in this mysterious hole in the Pieniny. Perhaps it was the entrance to some cave system that extends under the Pieniny.

The next was a letter from our number one Theoretician of Polish Ufologia - **Krzysztof Piechota,** MA from Warsaw, who has a slightly different view on the whole matter:

It is not a thankful task - an attempt to assess something that you did not deal with yourself, and unlike Maciej Kuczyński, my knowledge of the caves is poor, although the charms of several of them affected me closely. One thing I know for sure, namely that you need a real imagination to make a small thing great - it's an excursus into the theory of Prof. Jan Pająk about the glassy walls of some tunnels allegedly formed after flights of UFOs through the interiors of orogens. The thing is that I know the nature of this phenomenon like few others do and that is why a similar assessment on the impact of UFOs on the environment would never occur to me. One thing, however, I can say for sure – I'm full of praise and admiration for the author for pointing out that it is possible to build a flying object with a magnetic drive, i.e. magnocraft. It seems possible, but an object with such a propulsion source will have little to do with UFO, because the latter are not artificial creations, built on the model of terrestrial vehicles. I write about it here to point out that UFO as a short-lived and peculiar phenomenon of nature, certainly has nothing to do with the creation of the Moon Cave or other similar creations and rock formation processes. Returning to the assessment of the search for the Moon Cave, one can say it – the pursuit of this ephemera by its very definition seems to be barren, because it is difficult to count on success where one thesis is attempted to build up with further hypotheses. In a word, we are dealing here with a conglomerate of hypotheses and nothing more. There are no tangible traces, subsequent threads suddenly appear and disappear almost immediately, and this also applies to artifacts from previous civilizations, which were allegedly lost although in reality they never existed. They were made up. Is it similar with the Moon Cave?

Many strange caves exist in the world and some fragments may indicate that they were made artificially, using a sophisticated technique. However, in the case of caves, it is similar to many other movable artifacts - an adjective suggesting their artificial creation is added to the real feature; if, for example, a fragment of the artifact, in this case a section of the cave wall is extremely smooth - then it is enough to use the ambiguous term, e.g. the adjective - "glassy" to give it the appearance of an artificial creation, made at high temperature, in turn an enigmatic term "trough in yellowish sandstone" gives the appearance of a regular formation with flat and even walls; sometimes one word evokes an avalanche of associations, which in turn are connected with other artifacts attributed to the activities of intelligent beings, and their enumeration creates the illusory impression of abundance and strangeness that applies to lost civilizations. Similarly, was made the mystery of the phenomenon of UFO, whose name it got in the era of earthly flights of aircraft, is used to invariably and wrongly describe the alleged vehicles of alien civilizations from space that supposedly came to Earth.

Well, it seems that in the case of the Moon Cave, the problem has been exaggerated too much – it was assigned a range of data that the imagination of the authors dictated them, and not experience or exploration of underground creations of nature. On the other hand, after all, natural caves exist, and because man has not yet invented anything that nature would not have created before, at an early stage of his cultural development he also began to drill rocks, not only the caves with connecting corridors but even huge underground buildings and entire cities. It was happening at a time when no one had thought that stone could be cut and modeled in a fancy way, allowing the construction of buildings – free-standing or habitable homes. However, it was not a sophisticated technique, using a laser or sandpaper, as there was no such need. The vast majority also used natural creations, often giving the impression that they didn't come from this world. There are so many breathtaking caves in the world, where the average mortal will never reach, because it requires the difficult skill of diving with an oxygen apparatus or traveling through such long, narrow and winding underwater passages that it is a venture only for daredevils with extremely healthy lungs. Many of these caves could be called Moon Cave. However, do such caves exist in the Polish mountains, in the Beskids or the Sudetes? Perhaps. After all, nothing is impossible in this world.

From the information available to me, it appears that counting on a geological scale, not so long ago, after the retreat of the flood waters, which was associated with the fall of some civilization called Atlantis, which picked all the fruit from the "tree of knowledge," significant sections of the human population inhabited labyrinths of caves, which often were connected by underground corridors. Perhaps this fact, together with memories of the bright past, decided that not only in ancient times but also today are mentioned underground cities and entire kingdoms, many of which may have deserved to be called legendary Agartha. It is possible that modern hypotheses and theories refer to those not too distant in time but due to the censorship extremely vague information. The important thing is that these and similar attempts to reach the historical truth don't turn into imaginary theories without any coverage in facts.

In the light of the information cited in the study, it will certainly be extremely difficult to justify the existence of the exotic Moon Cave, which is sought in a relatively well-known area. Let's look at it from the other side - after all, the beginnings of Poland were equally legendary and yet more and more archeological discoveries confirm the fact that the beginnings were real. This doesn't mean that Poland existed before it was established, but that's not the point. It is important to never stop searching.

Krzysztof Piechota
Warsaw, July 23, 2003

That's all from our Number One.

The next was a letter from the already mentioned **Olaf Snappan** from Zabrze, who is the author of a huge monograph entitled "Zwierciadło wiadomości" also dedicated to the history of Humanity. It reads as follows:

[...] you write about artifacts from millions of years ago and about alleged Interterrans. Well, I would like to say that you need to be very careful in dating finds from before the global cataclysm, the Deluge, the Atomic War of the God. - i.e. being more than 12-13 thousand years old. Why? Well, all these calculations completely don't take into account atomic explosions, or even a flood in a given area. Therefore, it may shock a scholar or student that the bones of some American sauropods dated 70-80 Ma ago may not be true.

So, if 12-13 thousand years ago there was a conflict with the use of atomic weapons, and then a geological catastrophe, all these methods of dating based on radionuclides aren't worth a hoot.

I will give an example: the remains of sauropods may not be 80 Ma old, but only 22-28 thousand years. Hans Zillmer writes about this in detail in "Darwin's Mistake" and "Największe Pomyłki w Dziejach Ziemi." If we accept our theory of atomic prehistory, then:

- *petrified shoe prints in Corfu are not 1 Ma old, but for example 15 thousand years old;*
- *clay figurine from Nampa is not 2 Ma old, but e.g. 20 thousand years old;*
- *stone pestle from Mt. Table is not 9 Ma old, but 20-25 thousand years old;*
- *the chalk sphere from Laon is not 40 Ma old, but e.g. 30-37 thousand years old;*
- *petrified footprints on a stone in Martin can be 13 thousand years old;*

- *the nail from Kingoodie is not 387 Ma old, but just slightly over 40 thousand years old;*
- *metal vase from Dorchester certainly isn't 600 Ma old, but maybe about 1 Ma - 30 thousand years old;*
- *the corridor system in the Owl Mountains cannot come from pre-human times and be 400,000 years old.*

I give all these dates based on the calculation that e.g. the flood or atomic wars have changed the content of many elements in nature and you can't date very many finds using old methods.

Of course, there could have been some First Generation, but it probably was a few million years ago, because the evolutionary dating of the Cambrian and Precambrian Period (Charles Lyell School in 1833) is now obsolete (at least for us). On the other hand, you can't say how old the Earth is – maybe Earth's time is a snake devouring its own tail.

Personally, I'm inclined to the sober thesis of Mr. Krzysztof Piechota, although it seems to me that some UFOs are artificial.

Zabrze, September 29, 2003

One of the most interesting mysteries of prehistory is located in northern Slovakia. Already in 1967, wrote about it, the dean of Czechoslovakian SF literature - **Dr. Ludvík Souček** (1926-1978) - he wrote about strange footprints found near the village of Konské in the Martin poviat, and he returns to this problem in his book 'Tušenie súvislostí' with the words:

The indentations in the limestone boulders have an exact shape and exactly match the human footprints, which is particularly well seen in the three best-preserved footprints, the others are already damaged by erosion. These feet correspond to the shape and size of the human foot of a Homo sapiens, and therefore not a Neanderthal, what is more, they are footprints of a man who often walked barefoot, as indicated by fingerprints. Anthropologists from Prague and Bratislava stated, after examining the traces in 1960, that these prints are authentic and that a man whose legs imprinted in the rock couldn't walk the world 100,000 or even 50,000 years ago.

Examination of the rock gave a shocking result because on the basis of guide fossils the time of formation of these limestones was estimated - they were formed in the older Tertiary - about 50 Ma ago. At this time, you can't even talk about homo sapiens walking the Earth.

That's all from Dr. Souček.

(Souček L. : "Tušenie súvislosti," Bratislava 1984, p. 36-37)

This village began to interest us after we came across an article by **Eng. Ivan Milan** "Fertilized feet," in which he showed the sad fate of these footprints in the limestone. For local peasants from Konskie, these prints were treated as taboos and nobody touched them. They were referred to as Janosik's footprints (and the reader should know that **Janosik aka Janošik** is a real historical figure, not a romantic hero from the humorous series of **Jerzy Passendorfer** from 1973.) But in the 1980s, the structure of agriculture changed – from small plots to large plantations of intensive cultivation of various industrial plants. The boulders with traces were pushed with bulldozers 200 m below and turned to the ground. The traces were perfectly preserved by wetland soil.

We wrote to Eng. Milan and a month later we received a response from the Board of the Protected Landscape Park Velka Fatra, where he worked. In the letter of April 25, 1989, we read the following:

I read about these traces in Dr. Souček's book and I'm surprised that I have not heard of them before. I was glad that such a thing exists and not far away from me. I was lucky to see them, write an article about them and do something for their case. What I saw there scared me a bit. I tried to turn one of these boulders, but without the help and tools I wasn't able. I didn't even know if there were any footprints on this stone. So, I left them, and I hope that one day I will be able to examine them thoroughly.

On May 15, 1989, together with Eng. Milan we went to Konskie. The incriminated boulders were located 700 m from the village, in a thicket of bushes. Based on the stories of the oldest inhabitants of the village, we selected the largest boulder with a circumference of 4 meters. Unfortunately, we didn't determine anything, because the traces were pressed into the soil. We also failed to examine the cave system, which hasn't been explored to this day, in the massif of the nearby Kopa peak - 1,187 m a.s.l. (the Kopa massif is perfectly visible from the road 70 near Kral'ovany). The other boulders were several hundred meters further and lower, and access to them was significantly impeded.

On June 3, 1989, we wrote a letter to Eng. Milan, in which we outlined partial research tasks of this problem:

- The boulder field survey;
- Collect all information from the oldest inhabitants of the village about these traces;
- If possible, enter the Kopa cave system and look for further traces of this kind. (Jesenský M. : "Rok archeologickej utópie," "Archeoastronautický sborník. Ročenka Československé archeoastronautické asociace za rok 1990," Centrum Čs.AAA, Prague 1990, p. 140-150)

The words were put into action and the boulders were turned using heavy equipment. Unfortunately, no trace was found on either of them. Nevertheless, one of the inhabitants showed him another boulder. Eng. Milan writes about this:

We also went there. Indeed, three feet were imprinted in the limestones. Three years ago, some employees from Bran made three plaster casts. However, it didn't calm me down at all. I can't believe that these are exactly the ones Dr. Souček mentioned. He wrote about "adult" and "children's" prints, and here I saw only "children's" ones and such less visible. So, I still believe that these footprints that Dr. Souček wrote about are still waiting for their discoverer.

I don't have any information about the cave in Kopa and I don't know anyone who would know where this cave is.

However, we were convinced not only about the existence of these traces, but also about the existence of the cave in Kopa. We got on the trail, despite the nasty and unfavorable weather conditions. It rained nonstop for two days, then the sun came out, but it was still wet.

On the first day, we found the rock about which Eng. Milan wrote. The indentations were not very clear; already devoured by erosion. On the second day, we searched the whole city. It was something terrible, we were wading in wet, waist-high grass and in constant rain. We broke through brushwood, with a notebook in our teeth. During the day, we penetrated 196 m^2 .

The result was negative.

On the evening of the second day, three young people came to our camp and we talked with them about the footsteps. We learned that these three prints were the ones the researchers dealt with. We returned to the camp and cleared the tracks. We were able to see heel marks and fingerprints. In addition, we managed to find four traces: three "children's" and one "adult." Left of the trail No. 4 there was a series of hollows – indistinct footprints the length of the step of the man who left them was 65 cm, so the "inventory" was as follows:

Track No. 1 - 21 cm long, it contains an interesting fingerprint that creates an obtuse angle with the other fingers. However, it seems that it is simply a limestone loss. The foot is small, as if childish. It has 5 fingers, but its size is increased by erosion. The heel is not impressed, but the fingerprints are clearly visible.

Track No. 2 - length 27 cm, it is longer, and it can be called an "adult" foot. The foot is well imprinted, all five toes are clearly visible.

Track No. 3 - 22 cm long, 5 fingers clearly visible, "childish."

Track No. 4 - 23 cm long, one finger clearly visible, the others are not clear.

All marks are devoured by erosion, and the latter one is cut by three crevices, which are located parallel to the direction of the march.

All traces are on a 220 x 230 x 140 cm boulder, there is also a 60 x 60 cm cut made artificially. On the next boulder is something like a handprint of some hominid. All this confirmed that these traces are only one small link in the entire chain of mysterious traces from the distant past. The work of Dr. A. Amannijazov, director of the Geological Institute of the Turkmen SSR Academy of Sciences from 1986, fell into our hands. The third expedition, which he led, discovered dinosaur traces in Khodja Pil Ata and human traces between them.

In his work (Amannijazov K.: "Sliedy Słońov svjatogo diedie," "Wokrug swieta," No. 10/1986) he writes as follows:

At one point, my attention was drawn to strange depressions on a rock slab, a little aside from the chain of dinosaur footprints, running parallel to them. As I approached them and looked at them well, it became clear that they weren't dinosaur tracks. Whose, then? One of the clearest traces resembled. I looked at my silent colleagues and realized that we were all thinking the same.

The petrified trail was similar to a footprint of a human, actually, of a human-like creature.

"Length 26 cm," measured and announced Vitaly Ivanovich.

"Size 43," said Oleg, "that is not very high."

"Don't forget to photograph them," I stopped him, "it's not yet the time for conclusions."

Of course, about our discoveries, we informed **Erich von Däniken**, whose address we obtained with difficulty (it was 1989), and the information was sent to the headquarters of the *Ancient Astronaut Society* in the Swiss Feldbrunnen on December 12, 1989, and was immediately enriched with further details.

Meanwhile, a new expedition was organized with the help of the Košyce *451 F* club and took place on October 20-21, 1989. The problem was immediately attacked from two sides: the first group went to the boulders in Konskie, while the second one went in search of a cave on Kopa.

The effects were interesting – the head of the club Dr. Martin Schuster gave us collected material from conversations with old people who lived there, who told him about prints of foot, hand and even whole body that were on the stones lying in this area. Those who studied the higher parts of the forest talked about more boulders, but they didn't find any prints, because the rocks were covered with fallen leaves. Soil and rock samples were taken and intended to be further examined and dated. Unfortunately, no entrance to the cave system of Kopa was found. This system, however, may exist, because Kopa is made of carbonate rocks, and only in such karst phenomena occur, so the existence of the cave system can be considered a foregone conclusion. If it were otherwise, it would be a deviance of Nature. We remind all opponents that recently two more chambers of the known to people caves in Červené vrchy have been discovered, where it seemed that everything had already been discovered and nothing new could be found. So, right are **Athanasius Kircher** (1601-1680), **Georg Bauer-Agricola** (1494-1555) and also **Taylor Sir**

Edward Burnett (1832-1917) who wrote this about it: *If we could penetrate Earth from pole to pole, or from our feet up to the antipodes, inside we would see with horror the pile terribly riddled with crevices and caverns.*

Therefore, it was decided to continue the search for all possible information about prints in libraries, archives and in the field. The same was decided regarding the Kopa cave system.

Rock samples have given strange results. The rock turned out to be relatively "young" and was, according to experts, 1.8 million to. 5,000-10,000 years old. Two samples were tested - one from a boulder and the other from the footprint with three slits. The results of the expertise showed:

The tested sample comes from the Mesozoic Era, i.e. from the period which was 230-65 Ma ago. It is a Mesozoic limestone, in this case, dolomite, which has identical chemical composition.

The tested fraction is weathered and porous, it is 1.8 Ma old, although the most likely age here is 5-10 thousand years. It is a form of limestone that arose as a result of the action of water saturated with CaO and MgO, passing through the Mesozoic limestone and flowing to the surface of the Earth.

This is some abracadabra, and it's hard to believe this opinion. Therefore, it will be necessary to repeat the dating of this limestone, because the data obtained are in sharp contrast to the facts:

- Dr. Souček claims that these rock formations - according to geologists - originate from the early Tertiary and must be millions, not thousands of years old.
- As you know, the hilly and mountainous surface of this massif with an area of 234 ha and a height of 437-864 m a.s.l. form tertiary sandstones, shales, and Mesozoic rocks.

- The local (western) slope is made of Mesozoic limestones, which stands in unpleasant contradiction with the experts' estimate quoted above.

In addition to the information of Dr. Souček included in his book, we managed to find only one information about the find in Konskie, which took place in the early 1990s.

In the journal "Slovensky kras," there was the article by Eng. Bart "Ten years of speleological research of the Institute of Archeology SAV in Nitra," where at 1961 there was a note about a "limestone slab with a human footprint." The author of the article was in Konskie in 1961, where a resident showed him a limestone slab with an impression of a huge human foot. Unfortunately, in an interview with Dr. Schuster, Eng. Bart said it was only an artifact that was created by surface erosion. In addition, he negated the position of the Konskie residents, claiming that there had never been any human footprints in the rocks. He assumed that human traces in the rock couldn't exist - and yet we know that nowadays still numerous finds are being discovered that don't match the official knowledge of our prehistory and have given all geologists, paleontologists, and anthropologists sleepless nights . for decades.

Of course, he didn't know anything about the boulder, he didn't know anything about archeological finds in the area, and of course the Kopa cave system. In conclusion, he added that IA SAV in Nitra is not going to deal with this matter and undertake any search in this area. Then he warned us not to do anything there and to forget about the whole matter as soon as possible.

None of the institutions we addressed were interested in this matter and distanced themselves from it. Nevertheless, regardless of whether we get the proverbial *nihil obstat* from them or not, research in this area will be conducted. We have such an attitude as E. and C. Ullman, who in their book "Mysteries of the Ancients" wrote:

Whether we like it or not, we must move some sacred cows of archeologists, anthropologists, and historians. We know that we will be criticized and persecuted. But examining the truth, we must sacrifice some sacred cows.

But that's not all, because there is one more aspect of the matter, well, scientists seem not to take into account one more thing, namely the fact that the feet of these people have imprinted in the white, limestone sand lying on the shore of the Tethys Ocean, which then fossilized forming limestone rocks: dolomites, gypsum, and marl. The geological history of the Carpathians indicates that these traces cannot be older than 65 million years, but they also cannot be younger than 22.5 - 5 million years - because at that time the Tethys Ocean closed and disappeared from the surface of the globe (its traces are part of the Mediterranean, the Black Sea, and the Persian Gulf), and this is what we owe to, deposits of salt, gypsum, sulfur, potassium salt, etc. As researches of scholars show, at that time the first people were just entering the savannas of Africa and they couldn't live in Central Europe. So, the dating provided by scientists from SAV leaves (to put it mildly) a lot to be desired, and all models of anthropogenesis and the spread of people across the planet are simply useless.

The Tertiary is the youngest and, as **Daniel Jarząbek** wrote, *the latest discovered of the lost landscapes*, which we, enchanted by visions of great Mesozoic reptiles, have not noticed for decades, and its history contains serious gaps and riddles. The most interesting of which in Slovakia are: the strange Cyclop Shield found in the Low Tatras suggesting that it is the remains of some machine from at least several hundred thousand years ago, mysterious stone balls and spherical negatives that were found in Kysuce (and recently in Silesian Beskids, near Węgierska Górka.), mysterious caves of the Orava Beskids or meteorites-spectra, which weren't meteorites at all.

Of course (here *polonicum*) the tunnel in Babia Góra described by **Dr. Eng. Jan Pająk** in his works and the mysterious Moon Cave. The latter - according to one version - may be located somewhere in the Šíp massif - 1,169 m, or in already mentioned here Kopa or in the ridge of Havran - 915 m, between the villages of Párnica and L'ubochňa, and is an artifact of the Platonic civilizations of Atlantis or Atlantica, at least 13,000 years old.

CHAPTER 11

Lux ex Oriente.

Petroglyphs in the Urals: Stone Age chemical formulas? - Meeting with Dr. Avinsky - Riddle of the Karelian stone book - About a witty traveler and secret signs in Siberia - The latest discovery of Bashkir scholars: An aerial map of the Mesozoic?

Gennady Chernenko is one of the Russian authors and at the same time seekers of answers to questions about ancient civilizations. This text was written based on the article "Уралские» писаницы" - отголоски визитов пришелцев?" In "Калейдоскоп НЛО" No. 1-2 [166], 2001. Here is one of the problems he has pointed out to the reader:

In the Urals, on the banks of the Tagil, Neyva, Rezh and Yuryuzan rivers (see map), you can see *pisanice* - drawings that were created on stones with ocher, supposedly mixed with blood. Their colors range between bright red, red-purple and brown. The thickness of the line is between 10 and 20 millimeters.

These drawings - according to specialists - were made about 4-5 thousand years ago. Some scholars took these drawings as some unknown form of writing, others - as secret signs. Either way, they aroused interest.

The rock inscriptions in the Urals have been known for a long time. Tsar Peter I in 1699 ordered his official - **Yakov Losiev** to go to this country, find a mountain with these drawings and copy them: *word for word – without any differences or changes - absolutely exactly.*

Already in our time they have been described and classified in the two-volume work of the archeologist **W. I. Cherniecov** entitled, "Rock drawings in the Urals." Archeologists came to the conclusion that the drawings depict hunting spells and secret signs of shamans, sorcerers, etc. That's true, because, in one of the drawings, we see a man standing next to a kind of cage with a wild animal inside. Hunting scenes are shown in many other drawings, but not in all. Many human figures were shown alone, not related to anything. When asked what these drawings represent, archeologists don't give a clear answer.

Geologist and mineralogist, **Dr. Vladimir Ivanovich Tyurin-Avinskiy** of Samara, is completely convinced that our planet was in the past visited by representatives of extraterrestrial civilizations. **In his opinion, these strange Ural rock drawings are nothing but images of chemical formulas...** Every high school student knows this graphic method of showing chemical formulas, so-called "structural formulas" mainly used in organic chemistry. These formulas consist mainly of branched chains and polygons - as can be seen in the figure.

And indeed - such zigzag lines with offshoots are found in rock drawings on the banks of the Neyva and Tagil rivers. What is that? Fishing nets? Archeologists disagree with this view:

"There is no evidence that there is a connection between these figures and fisheries," writes Cherniecov, "all the more so that not once have the images of fish in these drawings been found. Strangely these drawings remind structural patterns of all well-known polyethylene."

Here is another figure from the rock drawings found on Borodinské skály, on the river Rezh. The drawing resembles a honeycomb. Indeed - bees construct their combs from hexagonal cells, and here they are stretched vertically. But why old people didn't draw a single bee next to them? Archeologists can't explain the meaning of this drawing, while Dr. Tyurin-Avinskiy saw in the drawing the structural formula of graphite.

Finally, another rock drawing in the shape of a circle with "projections" or "offsets," which resembles quite accurately, the structural formula of the Gramicidin S antibiotic.

The Stone Age man couldn't know the symbols of modern organic chemistry – that's for sure. Dr. Tyurin-Avinskiy writes:

Primitive man didn't need to know them. All cave drawings in the Urals are associated with modern chemical symbolism: between these "pisanice" you can find fragments of hydrocarbon chains and stretched hexagons of benzene circles.

The scholar created the bold hypothesis that these chemical formulas could once have been passed on to primitive people by the newcomers from space who once visited Earth. He writes:

If the association of "stone patterns" with modern chemical formulas proves to be a fact, shouldn't these "pisanice" be considered a part of scientific luggage, which somehow became the object of worship of former inhabitants of the Earth?

Dr. V. I. Tyurin-Avinskiy showed copies of the cave drawings to physicists and chemists, and many of them agreed that they are very similar to chemical formulas.

If what Gennady Chernenko and Dr. Vladimir I. Tyurin-Avinskiy wrote about is true, and what I don't doubt, it may mean that we are either dealing with artifacts of Paleocontact which took place about 5-7 thousand years ago, or – which is most likely – we are dealing with artifacts of the powerful Scientific and Technical Supercivilization that existed until 10,000 BC and for unknown reasons disappeared. I see no sense in this that the Aliens provided people with knowledge that the latter couldn't understand, but I see the sense in transmitting and cultivating the memory and knowledge of the existence of a great civilization – e.g. the civilization of Atlantis, Lanka or Mu – which has disappeared or been destroyed in an internal global conflict – or maybe even inter-civilization one.

There are many cave drawings in Russia – for example, in the Sayan Canyon of the Yenisey, where scientists have found strange drawings of "mushroom people" who have a strange effect on animals and have a really "unearthly" appearance. (See Znicz-Sawicki L. – "Goŝcie z Kosmosu? – Paleoastronautyka" vol. 1, Gdansk 1980, p. 261-264). Were they aliens? Perhaps, but wouldn't it be easier to assume that they were simply people dressed in strange suits and equipped with apparatus weird for their artists? Here is another strange association – in the Ural and Sayan mountains there are deposits of uranium-thorium ores.

Strange drawings of spaceships and unusual "beings" are also found in the Fergana Valley (today Uzbekistan). Is it a coincidence that there are uranium ore deposits in the area? The appearance of Aliens got associated with the surroundings of uranium-thorium ore deposits already in the years 1944 – 46 by the famous Soviet fantasy writer, geologist, and paleontologist, **Prof. Dr. Ivan A. Yefremov**, which he expressed in the book "Stellar Ships" and the collection of short stories "White Horn."

We had the opportunity to meet the author of the unusual hypothesis about Ural *pisanice* in September 1996 during the 2nd International Ufological Conference in Debrecen, where we exchanged views, among others on the ecological aspect of ufology. Returning to discoveries in the Urals, we believe that similar discoveries should also be found in Central Europe, especially where there are deposits of uranium and thorium ores: in the Sudetes and the Świętokrzyskie Mountains. Let's hope that in this context some of the secret signs known from the Tatra and Pieniny "spiski" will find their new, how surprising explanation. If someone wants to look for them, I recommend reading the books of Dr. Jacek Kolbuszewski from Wrocław, who devoted several works to them.

Now another flower from the garden of unusual discoveries:

In the spring of 1960, an employee of one of the Karelian collective farms discovered mysterious drawings on the smooth coastal stones of Lake Onega. Interested in his find, on the next day off he went on a trip around the lake. It turned out that there are a huge number of such drawings. The strange "gallery of drawings" stretches for 20 km. Particularly a lot of drawings are found on two capes on the lake: Biesov Nos and Pieri Nos. This discovery is discussed in an article by **Yuri Lyubimov**, which appeared in the weekly "Калейдоскоп НЛО" No. 24 (291)/2003 of June 6, 2003.

After some time, an archeological expedition arrived on the banks of Onega. It soon turned out that rock drawings (petroglyphs) such as on the shores of this lake are also found on the shores and some islands of the White Sea. Over time, archeologists discovered more and more new drawings. Currently, over 1,000 mysterious paintings have been discovered on the shores of Onega, and over 2,000 on the shores of the White Sea. Archeologists called them the pages of a stone book or a gallery of works of art. Indeed, the stone images of the old masters present us not only the life but also the thoughts of these ancient people of the Mesolithic period (i.e., the period covering 8,000 - 4,800 BC).

Sometimes it seems that these drawings contain some encrypted messages, however, we are not yet able to read them, due to the ignorance of the code or the cipher key. Scientists believe that Karelia's petroglyphs turn out to be complex symbols that contain images and knowledge of ancient Karelians about the world around them.

From all this, it follows that the former artists created their paintings on the surface of boulders hitting them with pieces of quartz. Not very deep lines were obtained - about 2 mm. Along with hunting and fishing scenes, there were also strange episodes: some creatures roughly resembling people, holding in their hands some ritual utensils whose purpose is completely incomprehensible to scholars. Drawings of human and animal figurines are small - their length is 5 cm, although there are also huge ones - up to 4 m high. The most interesting, however, is that these figures can be seen best when illuminated by the diagonal rays of the rising or setting sun. Mysterious sculptures and lunar and solar signs are particularly visible at such moments.

Sea and forest animals, water birds, people, boats, bows, arrows, harpoons – all these, old artists began to consolidate in stone about 6,000 years ago. Work in this "Karelian art gallery" was going for a very long time, at least for several dozen centuries. Archeologists, who are conducting excavations there, claim that petroglyphs appeared there along with the first traces of a settlement. Perhaps, these drawings were initially made in places of worship. It is no accident that they are in secluded places on the coast. They are so close to the water that it seems that the beings depicted on them have just come out of the depths or are descending into them. Some images are hidden underwater. When you approach the stones with the largest number of petroglyphs and look at the sides, it becomes clear - they are the contact points of the three worlds: air, earth, and underwater ones. It is in these places that the greatness of knowledge and necessity of communing with higher forces and mythical figures of the invisible world is felt. A man who is here feels the stimulation of vitality and mental strength. Archeologists have determined that the former temples were here long before the appearance of petroglyphs.

The dowsers determined with their instruments that there are strongly radiating energy zones in this area – hence the stimulation of vital forces in people – which have a positive effect on human organisms. Perhaps that is why the former Karelians, who didn't move too far from Nature and sensed the energetic rhythms of the Earth, chose these places for their temples. At first, infirm drawings made of charcoal or blood appeared on the stones, but the first downpour washed them. Therefore, the artists began to carve them in stones so that they would remain in them forever. The animals, people and mysterious, fantastic creatures depicted on the pages of the "stone book" became immortal and have been watched by subsequent generations including the current one. It was here that spring fertility and hunting rituals, initiations, sacrifices to the spirits of the Ancestors began.

It may be that the mysterious creatures depicted on the stones, only roughly reminiscent of people are just a figment of fantasy of ancient Karelians. It cannot be ruled out that there are real representations of events from distant millennia ahead of us. Whom do they present? So far, no one has been able to answer this question.

Scholars admit that the meaning of Karelian petroglyphs is a mystery to them. Unfortunately, modern man cannot look at these drawings through the eyes of his former ancestors. That's why the summary of the content of this "stone book" remains inaccessible to us.

On August 1, 2003, a Russian translator, journalist, and writer, Mr. **Vadim Konstantinowich Ilin** from St. Petersburg, contacted me about this matter and pointed out to me that in the light of the materials he possessed, the matter of Karelian petroglyphs was already investigated by Russian scholars in the first half of the nineteenth century. He also emailed me a copy of **Vladimir Levin**'s article "Рисунки эпохи каменного века на скалах Карелии," which in Poland appeared in the magazine "Dookoła świata" No. 29/1975, p. 5-6 under the Polish title "Pracownie świadomości."

V. Levin writes in the article that the petroglyphs were dealt with as early as 1848 when the conservator of the Museum of

Mineralogy **K. Grewingk** was sent by the Academy of Sciences and the Economic Society of St. Petersburg to the Arkhangelsk and Olonets Governorates to examine the state of the population in these regions of the Russian Empire. And here in one of the villages of Onega, he heard the story of "devilish signs" on the Biesov Nos Cape. He went there and saw Karelian petroglyphs, about which he then gave a lecture in St. Petersburg. Almost at the same time, a junior high school teacher **P. Szwed** came across the rock on Biesov Nos, who described his observations.

The next discovery took place after the November coup in 1925. A geography student from Saint Petersburg - **Aleksander Linieyev** - was shown in the village of Wygostron on the shore of the White Sea a huge rock covered with petroglyphs. It is Liniewskij who first examined these drawings - both from the White Sea and from Onega. In 10 years, he redrew and compared petroglyphs. This is a painstaking job.

According to the Soviet scientist - academician A. P. **Okladnikov** - these drawings were created during the change of farming from hunting and gathering to agriculture and breeding. Meanwhile, Linievskiy hypothesized that they are religious and magical.

Another scholar - **W. I. Ravdonikas** - believes that *not only do these petroglyphs reflect reality from the Stone Age, but they also recreate the unreal, fantastic world of the fairy tales and legends of the people who created them.* This gave rise to wide speculation on the content of individual "pages" of this "stone chronicle." The thought thrown by Ravdonikas was extended by another researcher K. D. Laushkin, who elevated it to the rank of a scientific hypothesis. He claims that *we are dealing with a giant temple of the Sun-God, where the dome is the sky itself, the altar - the horizon, and the sun - the living god.*

Petroglyphs have also been found on the islands of Shoyrukshin and Erpin Pudas on Onega and near the villages of Zawavruga and Novaya Zawavruga on the island of Bolshoi

Malinin in the White Sea. A total of 1,176 new petroglyphs were discovered, which is twice more than on Onega. Among them were as many as 428 drawings of boats.

According to the researcher of the Karelian petroglyphs **A. D. Stolar** - *these petroglyphs turn out to be not only a "chronicle" or "encyclopedia" of old life, but above all a kind of "workshop of consciousness" in which for millennia the spiritual values of humanity accumulated and were realized.*

It was written in the 1970s. But what can we say now, at the beginning of the 21st century? Personally, we are convinced that the Karelian "stone chronicle" presented a picture of what faced the survivors of the previous civilization, which ended with the flooding of Atlantis by the waters of the Great Deluge - or if you like - a giant tsunami. For us, this is another link in the long chain of evidence that we are not the first here. Because, let's look at a few links that were found only in the territory of the Russian Federation: a stone "map of the gods" from Ufa, "Ural Pisanice" by Dr. V. I. Tyurin-Avinskiy, rock drawings from the Sayan canyon of the Yenisei presenting "mushroom people," rock drawings from Yakutia - and now a "stone book" from Karelia. And they are all dated 10-6 thousand years BC. Is this just a coincidence? No, there are no such cases and there can't be.

On April 14, 1828, we set off from Irkutsk to the north-east, and at the beginning of June, after traveling a thousand versts, we reached Beredin's stanitsa. My friend, with a Doctor of Philosophy (Ph.D.), Shuperman, an excellent natural science expert, but a bad rider, was completely exhausted and couldn't continue his journey. One couldn't imagine anything more funny than the respectable representative of the natural sciences riding bent like a bow on a skinny horse and festooned from all sides with rifles, pistols, barometers, snake skins, thermometers, beaver tails, birds and animals stuffed with straw, and especially one hawk of unknown species which, due to lack of space on the chest and back, he put on his hat.

These words come from a short story of the forgotten Polish writer, traveler, and orientalist **Jan Józef (Osip) Sękowski** (1800-1858), written in Russian and published in 1833 in St. Petersburg under the title "Scholarly Journey to Bear Island." In it he provides information about the mysterious cave at the mouth of Lena, which was the purpose of their scholarly journey:

The doctor told me that at the mouth of Lena there is a cave, which Pallas and Gmelin who regretted that they failed to see it with their own eyes, tried to describe according to the accounts of Russian polar hunters. Our fishermen call it "Писанная Комната," Pallas uses the form "Pisannaja Komnata" (Pallas Reise v. II, p. 108), and Reiggnes translated it to German as "geschreibene Zimmer" (Reiggnes Reise, p. 218). And Gmelin organized a special expedition to discover and explore this cave. It was known already in the Middle Ages. Arab geographers who found out about it from the Kharasian merchants called it Gar-el-Kitabe, which means the Cave of Letters, and the island where it is located - Abd-el-Gar - that is, the Land of Caves. ('Origines Russes, extraits de divers manuscrits, orientaux, pai hammer', p. 56 - 'Memoire populorum', p. 317). Chinese universal geography, quoted after scholar **Klaproth**, says of it as follows:

Near the mouth of the Li-no River there is a cave on a high mountain with inscriptions in an unknown language that was found during the time of Emperor Yao. The scholar Min-Tsi claims that they cannot be read without the help of the grass that grows on Confucius' grave.

(Klaproth - "Abhandlungen uber die Sprache und schrift der Uiguren," p. 72. see also "Opisanije Džungariji and Mongoliji of Father Iakinta;" Senkovskij O. - "Vědecká výprava na Medvědí ostrov," Czech edition in: "Magický krystal," Prague 1982, p. 104, Polish edition entitled "Podróż uczona na Wyspę Niedźwiedzią" in the anthology "Polska Nowela Fantastyczna," Warsaw 1985, vol. 4).

Also, **Piano Carpini**, a 14th-century traveler in Siberia, mentions a strange and interesting cave lying in the last place in the north - literally: *in ultimo septentrioni*, as a place of inscriptions in the language spoken in Paradise. Sękowski visionarily speculates that it is about the Flood and lost cultures, which was caused by the impact of the comet. He does it in a humorous - satirical form, but the thought is healthy. In his innovation, he overtook atlantologists and scholars like **Walter and Luis Alvarez**, who in the collisions of the Earth with small (of course in a cosmic scale.) celestial objects see causes of the *Extinction Events*, but also the engine of evolution. A legitimate question arises: how did Sękowski come up with the idea for his story and Egyptian hieroglyphs on the inhospitable shores of the seas of the Russian Far North? The answer to this is now simple. Traveling around Russia, he could see mysterious rocks covered with petroglyphs on the shores of the White Sea, which then turn into the *Писанную Комнатъ* in the Lena Delta, on Bear Island. At least this puzzle has found its solution. What a pity that he is a writer completely forgotten in Poland.

So, we are dealing with another trail leading to continents and civilizations lost in the depths of time, and by no means the last.

This discovery of Bashkir scientists is an unpleasant crack and contradicts traditional views on human history. It is an old stone slab, at least 120 million years old with a relief map of the Urals. More accurate data on this discovery was provided by the online edition of the Prawda daily. We will get acquainted with it thanks to the editorial article of the Slovak quarterly "UFO Magazín" No. 2, 2002.

It seems impossible. Scholars from the Bashkir State University have obtained direct evidence of the existence of an ancient, highly developed pre-human civilization. It is about huge stone slab found in 1999. A map of the area was engraved in it using unknown technology. This is a relief map, very similar to today's military maps. There are visible 12,000 km long canal system, partitions and huge dams. Near the channels are some diamond-shaped objects (pyramids???), the purpose of which is unknown. The map also contains several text and digital inscriptions. Scholars first assumed that this was an Old Chinese script, but it turned out that these inscriptions were in some hieroglyphic-syllabic language of unknown origin. No one can read it so far.

"The more I delve into it, the more it turns out that I don't know anything," admits **Prof. Dr. Aleksander Huvyrov** from the BSU, meaning this sensational discovery. Already in 1995, together with a Chinese student **Huan Hun**, he published the hypothesis about the migration of ancient Chinese to Siberia and the Urals. During their expedition to Bashkiria, they found several stone inscriptions in Old Chinese, which confirmed their hypothesis about migration. Most of the inscriptions contained information about commercial matters, weddings, and funerals.

During their search, Dr. Khuvrov and Hun stumbled across the 18th-century document in the archives of the Governor of Ufa. It was about 200 unusual stone slabs, which were located near the village of Chandar in Nurimansk Oblast. So, they assumed that these slabs were related to the migration of ancient Chinese. Digging in the archives, they found further documents, which showed that at the turn of the seventeenth and eighteenth centuries the expedition of Russian scholars found 200 white, stone plates with unknown drawings and signs. At the beginning of the 20th century, archeologist **A. Schmidt** also spoke about these plates. Professor Khuvrov and his student soon began to look for mysterious stone tablets. In 1998, they called for a group of students to help. They even rented a helicopter and flew over the places where these plates were to be located. Unfortunately, they found nothing. Professor Khuvrov has already begun to think that the stories about stone slabs are only a beautiful legend.

However, everything changed by chance. During one of his visits to the village of Chandar, Dr. Khuvrov met with the former chairman of the local collective farm, **Vladimir Kraynov**. He asked him if he was the scholar who was looking for stone tablets. He said yes. "*I have one stone plate in my yard*," explained Kraynov. It was July 21, 1999. Dr Khuvrov went to Kraynov's house and indeed - there was a stone slab with some petroglyphs and drawings under the porch. It was so heavy that it couldn't be picked up. So, the professor went to Ufa for help.

After a week, work began in Chandar. After extracting the plate from the ground, researchers measured it accurately - it was 148 cm high, 106 cm wide and 16 cm thick. Its mass was about 1 ton. It was pulled out of the pit with wooden rollers. Dr. Khuvrov called the find the *Dashka Stone* from the name of Daria - his newborn granddaughter. It was transported from Chandar to the BSU, where it was thoroughly examined. When the clay and earth were removed, the scholars didn't believe their eyes. "*Already at first glance, it became clear that this is not an ordinary stone,*" Prof. Khuvrov said. "*It was a map, only not ordinary, but three-dimensional.*"

"*How did we find out what area it represents?*" explains the professor. "*Initially, we didn't think that it is so old. Fortunately, the relief of the earth's crust in Bashkiria hasn't changed much over several hundred million years, and so we could identify the Ufa Plain, which became the basis for our measurements. We made its geological profile and found its traces where the ancient map begins. Displacement of field points has its justification in the movement of tectonic plates, which in this case occurs from east to west. A group of Russian and Chinese experts in cartography, physics, mathematics, geology, chemistry and Old Chinese language, then said that the stone tablet contains a map of the Urals area with the Belaya, Ufimka and Sutolka Rivers.*"

Researchers also examined the geological structure of the *Dashka Stone*. It consists of three layers. The basis is hard dolomite. The second layer is a type of mineral enamel, which is a mystery to this day. In it, the map is carved. It is covered by a third, 2 millimeters protective layer of calcareous porcelain.

"It should be said here that the relief wasn't made by an ancient mason with any ancient tool," Prof. Khuvrov claims. *"It is completely impossible. I can say with the greatest certainty that the stone was machined."*

X-ray examination of the slab showed that it was made artificially with the help of very precise tools.

Initially, the scholars assumed that the plate was the work of ancient Chinese, and this is because there were vertical ideogram inscriptions. As you know, this type of writing appeared in China before the third century B.C. To check this hypothesis, Prof. Khuvrov visited the Imperial Library in China. He was allowed to stay in the archives for 40 minutes and there he flipped through some ancient manuscripts, but none of them contained anything similar to the inscriptions on the *Dashka Stone.* After consulting Huan's colleagues from the university, the hypothesis of the Old Chinese origin of this artifact was definitively rejected. In addition, scholars have proved that porcelain, with which the *Dashka Stone* was covered, was never produced in the Middle Kingdom. Attempts to decipher the inscriptions only led to the finding that they were dealing with hieroglyphic-syllabic writing. However, Dr. Khuvrov claims that he managed to read one of them – it is about the latitude at which today the city of Ufa is located.

The longer the scholars studied the plate, the more puzzles appeared. The map shows huge irrigation system. Next to the rivers, there are two artificial systems with canals 500 m wide and 12 artificial lakes, each of the size, 300 - 500 m wide, 10 km long and up to 3,000 m deep. To create them, there had to be moved - nay - 1,000 billion m^3 of soil. Compared to these objects, the Volga-Don canal looks like a miserable groove in the ground. According to Prof. Khuvrov, modern humanity is only able to do a small fraction of what *that* civilization could do. This map shows, for example, that Belaya River flowed initially in an artificial riverbed.

It was very interesting to determine the age of this artifact. First, the researchers measured the amount of the ^{14}C radioactive carbon, and then examined all layers of the slab using the so-called "Uranium clock," based on the decay of the $^{233,235,238}U$ atoms. The results were so different than the age of the table couldn't be calculated. Thorough examination revealed two shells on its surface. One of them was 500 Ma old (Middle Cambrian), the other 120 Ma (the boundary between Lower and Upper Cretaceous). This age of the table was adopted by the researchers as a draft. *"The map was probably made when the North Magnetic Pole was in Franz Josef Land* (this configuration of the NMP was in Tertiary, i.e. 65 - 1 Ma ago)," *claims Prof. Khuvrov. "Our map defies the traditional understanding of human history. At first, we thought it was 3,000 years old. We thought so until we discovered two shells that were inserted so that they marked real objects on the map. No one can guarantee that these shells were still alive or fresh when the map was made. The map creator could have used existing fossils for it."*

The most interesting, however, is the purpose of this map. It was examined at the Center of Historical Cartography in the state of Wisconsin (USA). American scholars were shocked. According to them, such a three-dimensional map could be used only for one purpose - to navigate. It could be made only thanks to the data obtained from a bird's eye view - from the air. Note, Americans are currently working on making such a three-dimensional map of the whole world, which will last until 2010. The problem is that when developing such a map, huge amounts of information should have been processed. *"Try to map for example these mountains,"* says Prof. Khuvrov, *"you will have to use supercomputers and photos taken from the shuttle."* So, who made this ancient map? Professor Khuvrov answers: *"I don't want to talk about the UFO or aliens. This unknown author of the map, I will name briefly - the Creator."*

It seems that the one who created this map was using air transport. There is no road visible on the slab, although waterways should be considered. It is also possible that he didn't live in a given area but prepared it to settle using an irrigation system.

Further research on the map has recently brought new discoveries and bold hypotheses. Scholars are now absolutely certain that this plate is a fragment of a huge plastic map of the whole Earth. According to some theories, there would be as many as 348 such tables, and they are located quite close to the place of the first find. In the vicinity of the village of Chandar, scientists examined 400 soil samples and came to the conclusion that the entire map was somewhere near Sokolský vrch. During the Ice Age, it fell to pieces under the influence of the glacier. If you could find them all, its dimensions would be 340 x 340 m. Based on archival materials, Khuvrov determined the probable locations of other four stone slabs. One of them would be located under one of the houses in the village of Chandar, the second under the warehouse of the merchant Hasanov, the third under the village bath (banya), and the last under the pillar of the local narrow-gauge railway viaduct.

Bashkir scholars have informed scientific centers around the world about this discovery, but no one was interested (as usual). Except for one case - namely, when the research was in full swing, on the table of Prof. Khuvrov appeared a small stone - chalcedony. There was a similar relief on it as on the stone slab. Apparently, someone saw this relief and wanted to copy it, but who and for what???

CHAPTER 12

A Visit to the Valley of the Dead

Yakutian roads of death, or legends about the land of destruction - Witnesses of desolation: natives, visitors, and Red Army soldiers - Atomic bunkers in Siberia? - Mysterious explosions and pillars of fire behind the Urals - Nuclear training grounds or prehistoric global defense system?

In the north-west of Yakutia, in the region of the upper course of the Vilyuy River, there is a difficult to reach land with traces of some terrible cataclysms: wide windthrow in old forests, as well as stone fragments scattered around, stretching for hundreds of kilometers. In this land, deep underground, there are inconceivable metal objects. Their presence is manifested on the surface only through patches of strangely growing vegetation, and these patches represent a great danger to people. The old name of this land was *Ewyuyu Chyerkyechyeh*, which means in Yakut, the *Valley of Death*.

Some mysterious objects in this land are also on the surface. One of them is a small, flattened and metal hemisphere, in which there are small metal rooms where even in the most severe frosts it is warm. In the past, several hunters rested in these rooms, but quickly contracted strange and severe diseases. If they spent several nights in a row there, they soon died. The village elders forbade people to go there and this place got forgotten. The second mysterious object was discovered by a geologist in 1936, and it looks like a metal hemisphere with very smooth walls emerging from the earth. The color of the metal is reddish, while the wall thickness is up to 2 cm. This hemisphere is slightly inclined, and you can get under it on a reindeer (Uvarov V. : "Strange constructions in Siberia," Nieznany Świat, No. 8 (92)/1998, p. 36-37 and 42).

A similar discovery was announced already in the nineteenth century by researcher **Viktor R. K. Maak** in his report, which reads as follows:

In Suntar they told me that in the upper reaches of Vilyuy, there is a small river called Angyj Temierit, which means "Great Cauldron Drowned." Not far from its shore, in the forest, there is a huge copper cauldron buried into the ground. Only its ridge comes out of the ground, so that its diameter is unknown, although they say that whole trees grow in it.

This fact was also noted by another researcher of ancient Yakutia cultures - **N. D. Arkhipov**:

In the middle of the Vilyuy river basin, there is the account of many huge brown boilers located in the upper reaches of this river, called "olguyev." This report deserves attention, and this is due to the fact that many local rivers bear in their names the Yakutian root "olguydakh" - "boiler."

And then the most unbelievable - an old nomad told me about some "metal hole" - in which lie "slim, huge, one-eyed people in iron clothes."

And now closer to our time, a local guide also mentioned that near the fire there was an "iron burrow" with "iron people."

When this case became famous, new testimonies and witnesses appeared. A hunter discovered under the ice a reddish metallic surface that belonged to a huge dome deeply embedded in the frozen ground. Two people were returning to the base after extinguishing a huge forest fire when under burnt trees they discovered a huge dome, 5-6 meters in diameter.

Local legends say that these inconceivable installations and buildings appeared "a long time ago." Large, round "iron houses" stand supported by powerful brackets. They have no windows or doors, only the top of the dome has a "wide hatch." There are also other objects - clusters of metal "canopies-hemispheres" and protruding from the ground "huge, triangular, metal spur," a la pyramid.

So, these descriptions can't be called fabrications, because there are eyewitnesses who have seen the objects described here. In the 1960s, a hunter went to the forbidden zone in the taiga and saw a cone broken in half, from whose side, there was sticking out a peculiar triangular object about 3 m long. Recently, the Yakut newspaper Edier SAAS published a letter from a Far Eastern inhabitant - **Mikhail Koriecki**, who stayed with his father in this area in 1933, 1939, and 1949, and who writes about it as follows:

As for the enigmatic objects, there are many of them, during three seasons I saw seven such "boilers" there. They are all a complete mystery: first of all, their sizes range from 6 to 10 m in diameter; secondly - they were made of some inconceivable metal, with which can't deal even our cutting tools, including a diamond saw. The vegetation around it is extremely lush - the grass grows above human height. Six of us spent one night in a "boiler." We didn't expect anything bad, but one of us lost all hair in a month, and on my head appeared three ulcers which I still have today. In addition, I found half the perfect black ball with a diameter of about 6 cm. It was smooth, literally slippery, like polished with an ideal tool. This strange "stone" cut the glass like a diamond.

In the 1950s, the military drew attention to this strange land and conducted research there, the results of which shocked specialists. It turned out that the military blew up some device,

with the explosion power 2-3 thousand times higher than assumed by their calculations. The concerned soldiers closed the area where these objects were and studied them for several years.

So, what can be said and how to analyze the information cited here? As you can see, we have here a rare mix of ancient legends and stories from the local population (these are testimonies from previous centuries up to the 1950s), and modern data about the **former nuclear training ground**. Only a new, well-equipped and managed expedition can explain this situation. Drawings of these extraordinary objects were made by the artist-painter **Yuriy Mikhailovskiy** based on eyewitness accounts (Psalomshchikov V. - "Mysterious hemispheres in Yakutia" in "Н Л О" No. 32 (145)/2000).

These three highlighted words in Dr. Psalomshchikov's article explain everything. Instead of the riddle of the abandoned city of the Foreign Scientific and Technical Civilization, we have an abandoned nuclear training ground - an object called Moscow-100, 200 or maybe 900. It's a pity that pseudo-ufologists make money on it, although not - in one respect, Valeriy Uvarov hasn't depart from the truth. Indeed, Aliens appear above the training grounds of weapons of mass destruction, which have long been proven by researchers **Prof. Jacques Vallée, Dr. Kiyoshi Amemiya** and others who deal with the issue of "UFO and the army."

Let's look at it from the other side. Let's assume that Valeriy Uvarov and the rest of his supporters are telling the truth, and that in the Siberian taiga, somewhere in the upper reaches of Vilyuy these mysterious objects are located, and the atomic training ground of the Soviet Army appeared only in the 1950s. This would mean that the area of the Central Siberian Upland, between 100° and 110°E and 64° and 68°N is the area, in which there are the artifacts of the Foreign Scientific and Technical Civilization, or - as we assume it - the remains of the Atlantean Supercivilization from at least 12,000 years ago. The phenomenon of the Tunguska Meteorite and also, the Tatra Moon Cave and the Tunnel in Babia Góra fit into all this. Of course, there are also orthodox explanations, namely in this region, there was a secret base where work on weapons of mass destruction was carried out in the times of the USSR. Another version says that there was a dump of burnt stages of carrier rockets launched from the Plesetsk Cosmodrome. Unfortunately, so far none of these versions have been substantiated.

And that's not all, because from the territory of the former USSR we are still receiving information about mysterious events, places, and artifacts that allow us to presume that we are not the first here and that our civilization is just one in a row. This territory is *terra nondum cognita* and we will hear about, read and see many more things (See also: **Nienacki Z.** - "Pan Samochodzik i człowiek z UFO," 3rd edition, Olsztyn 1991, Leśniakiewicz R. - "Walerego Uwarowa fantazje syberyjskie," "Czas UFO" No. 2/1998).

As we can see, conjecture won't help here - you need to organize an expedition into the taiga and examine the thing in situ, or - which will be cheaper and more effective, because you can see more from above – look carefully at satellite images of this area taken by American **Landsats** and French **Spots**. So, first the Internet search, and then, in the taiga. Perhaps there is a common denominator between El Dorado and the Vilyuy Death Valley – both were created in the course of the activities of the Atlantean Supercivilization. Just like the Moon Cave.

We hereby invite all Internet users to cooperate - instead of analyzing the noise of the radio gibberish of the Cosmos and supporting the senseless program SETI - it's better to deal with the analysis of satellite images of the Earth in search for real traces of action of alien reason, or *"those who were before us," because* it makes more sense than analyzing white cosmic noise, as it is certain that they are using something better than the radio and we have a chance to find signals of a civilization more primitive than us, or more or less at the same level. The search for such "death valleys" can lead to unexpected discoveries that push forward knowledge about our planet, civilization and above all history of the existence of *Homo sapiens* species on this planet. Anyway, we don't need to go that far. In our countries, we know a few places where strange things are happening and which would overshadow all those notorious curiosities in the West, which some authors from England, France, Spain or the USA write about. You just need to get out of the box of diagrams and the hammered into our heads, orthodox version of human history, determined by religions, ideology, and politics. But that's a topic for another narrative.

THE END

Krásno nad Kysucou - Jordanów,
April 26, 2004

ILLUSTRATIONS:

20.Rue de Rivoli Paris

Dr. Anthony Horak

001 – Capt. Dr. Antonin Horak – a hero of this story

002 – Mrs. Anna Horakova – his wife

à Mr le Pasteur Lagny.

C U R R I C U L U M   V I T A E .

Antonin Horak; né de parents Tchèques le 7 Juillet 1897 à Hermannstadt/Transylvanie (Austriche-Hongrie).
père Karel Horak , geomètre,
mère Maria née Kocher.

1903-07 école primair Tchèque à Prague/Karlin.

1907-15 école sécondaire = 4 premières classes Tchèques à l' école Real à Prague/Karlin , les 3 dernières classes Allemandes au Real-Gymnase de Prague/Karlin. J' ai passé les grandes vacances à Paris (6 mois en tout) et à Londres (4 mois en tout).

1915 examen final "Maturité".

1915-18 service militair dans l' armée de l' Autriche-Hongrie 1916 Officier de Résorve, degré final Prem. Lieutenant. Div décorations.

1918-19 Prem.Lieutenant dans l'armée Tchècoslovaque, occupation de la Slovaquie et "guerre" avec Hungrie-Bolshvique (Béla Kuhn).

1919-21 Academie Minière à Banska Stiavnica/Slovaquie, avec 2 semestres intérim à l' Academie de Leoben.

11 Octobre 1921 Diplom Ingénieur de mine de l' Academie Banska Stiavnica.

En Août 1921 mariage avec Anna,née Krisch.

1921-22 Deux semesters supplémentaires Université Prague. Diplom.

1922-25 ingénieur, technicien; dans saline Visakna/Transylvanie.

1925 6 mois en USA comme visiteur de mines.

1925-26 cours spécial de Geophysique Université de Prague. Diplom.

1926-30 directeur-adjoint ,mine Pribramy/Bohême.

1930-31 en USA, au Canada/Est, courtes éxcursions au Mexique -Chihuahua et Argentine-Goya; visiteur mines.

1932-35 directeur intérimaire Saline Vizakna.

1935-39 directeur mine Banska Bystrica/Slovaquie.

20/4 49
à Mr. Lagny.

1939-41 arreté par Allemands; Evadé du camp concentration "Theimwald" le 22 Juillet 1941.

1941-43 vie clandestine en Slovaquie.

1943-44 membre d' un groupe armé insurgés, secteur Podkarpatska Rus.

Février 1945 à Vizakna directeur (sous commandement Russe) de même saline où j' étais en 1935 et en 1925.

fine Mai 1945 fuite à Prague.

de fine 1945 à Prague au Ministère Trav.Publics comme conseill en matières minières ("Bansky Rada").

Décembre 1946 adjoint spécial au secteur minier de Jachymov (sous comm. Russe).

Mars 7 1948 fuite; depuis

Juin 1948 en France.Réfugié.

Ing.Ant.Horak.

003 and 004 – The Dr Horak CV (in French)

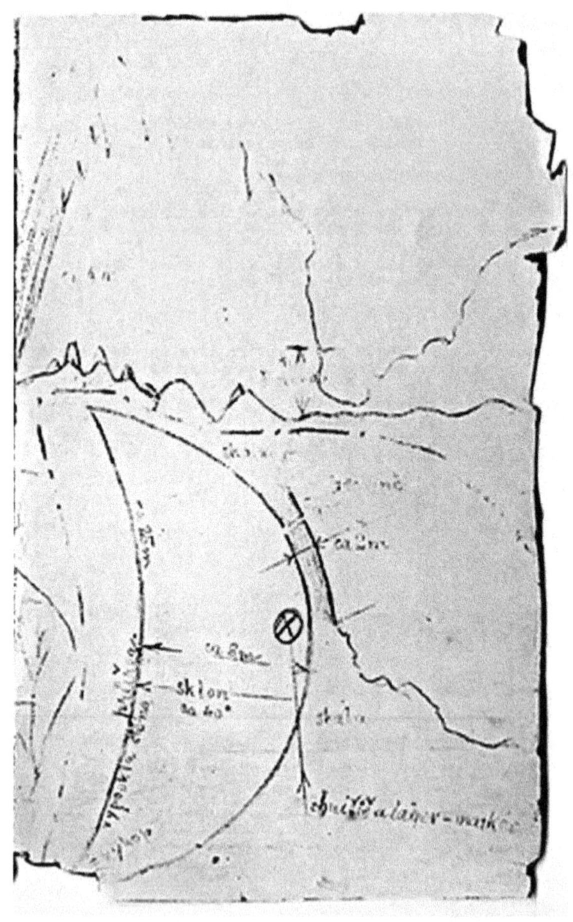

005 – Copy of the Dr. Horak's diary – a sketch of the Moonshaft

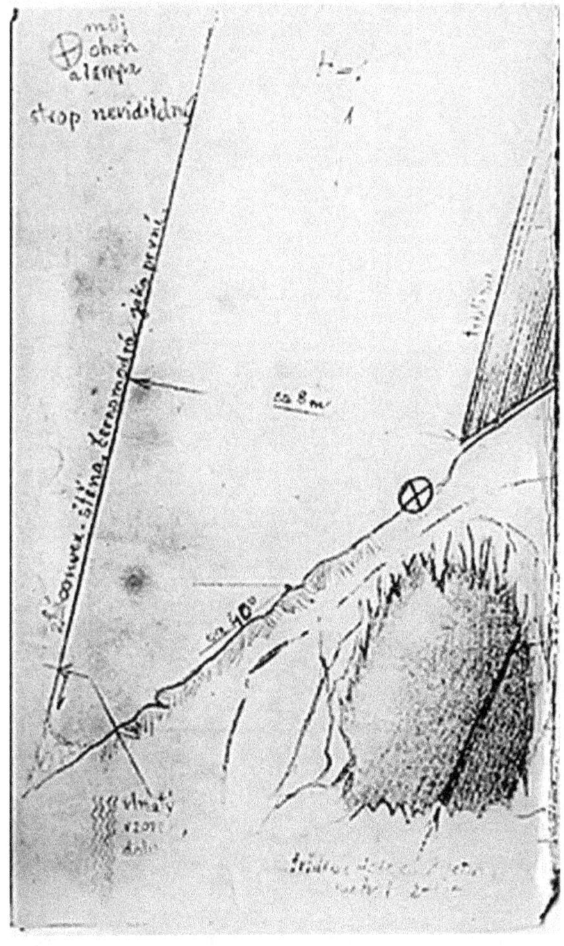

006 – Entry to the cave with the Moonshaft and a view of the shaft

007 – View on the mountains near the Moonshaft

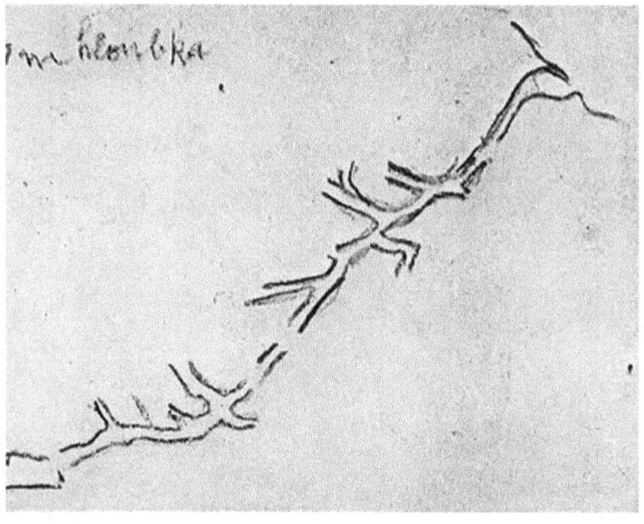

008 – Plan of the corridors of the cave from the Dr. Horak's diary

009 – Plan of the way to the Moonshaft cave

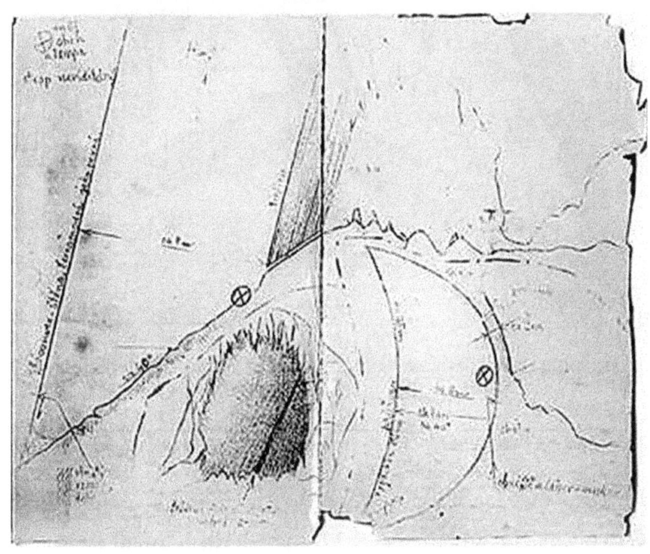

010 – The both pages of the Dr. Horak's diary

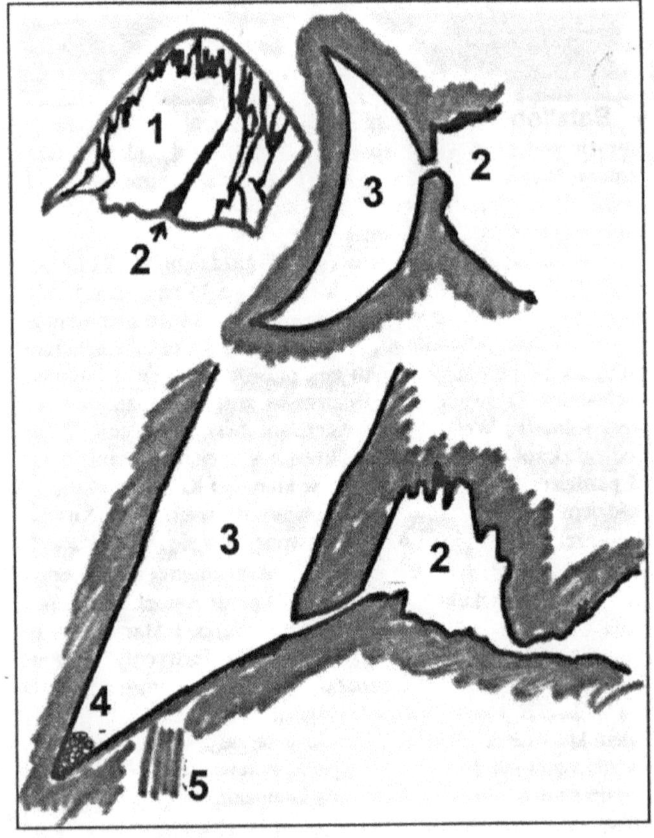

Drawing 3: 1. Metal wall, 2. The gap, 3. Half-moon shaft, 4. Regolith, 5. Cuts

011 – Drawings from the Thomas de Jean book: 1. Metalic wall; 2. Gap of the entry to the cave; 3. Moonshaft; 4. Small stones; 5. Slots in the Moonshaft floor.

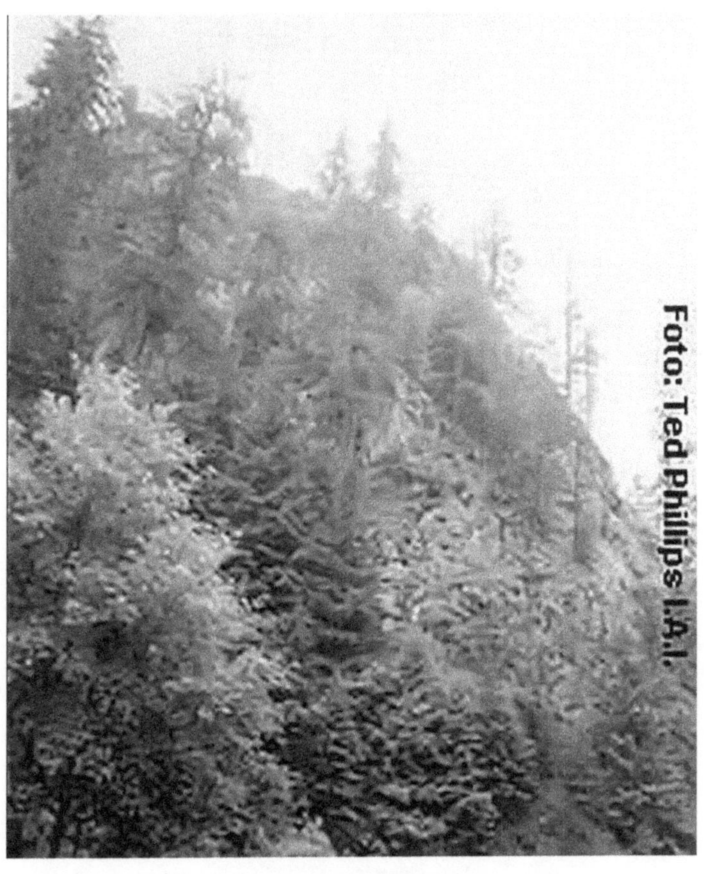

012 – Curved cliff near an entry to the Moonshaft cave (photo: Ted Phillips I.A.I.)

013 – An entry to the Moonshaft cave (photo: Ted Phillips I.A.I.)

014 – Mountain forest near an entry of the Moonshaft cave
(photo: Ted Phillips I.A.I.)

015 – Panorama of the Byelanskye Tatra Mts. (Tatry Bielskie, Belanske Tatry) from the Polish side

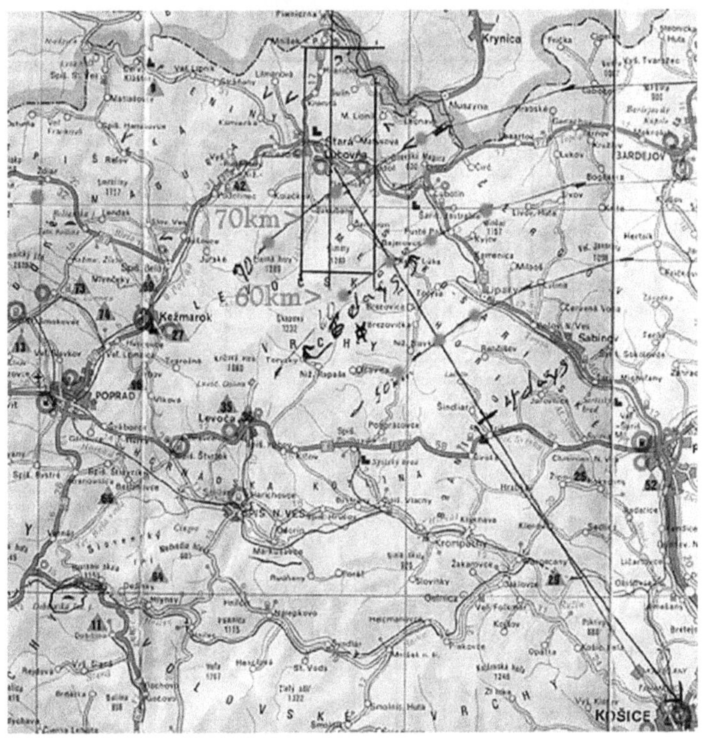

016 – Map of the distances among Stara Lubovna, Plavec and Kosice

017 – Map of the Moonshaft possible locations in Slovakia and Poland

018 – Map of the Moonshaft location in Slovakia. The Moonshaft possible is located nearby the Sulin village

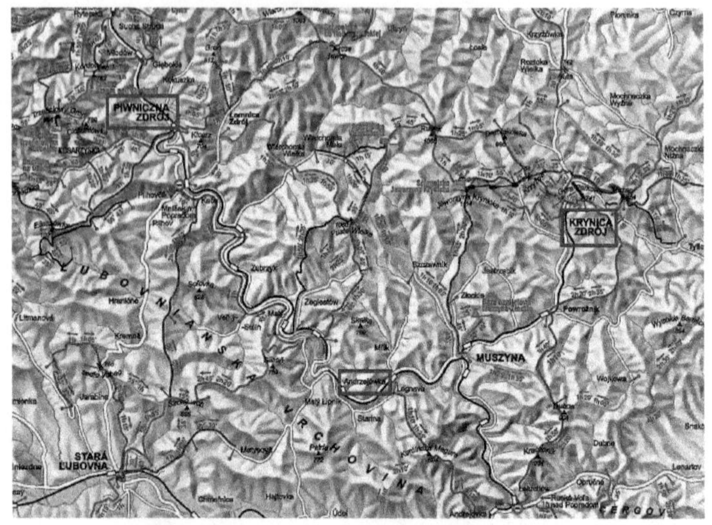

019 – Map of the Lubovnianska Vrhovina and Beskid Sadecki. The Moonshaft is located possible somewhere there – in the triangle among Andrzejowka, Krynica Zdroj and Piwniczna Zdroj in the Beskid Sadecki in the Polish borderland…

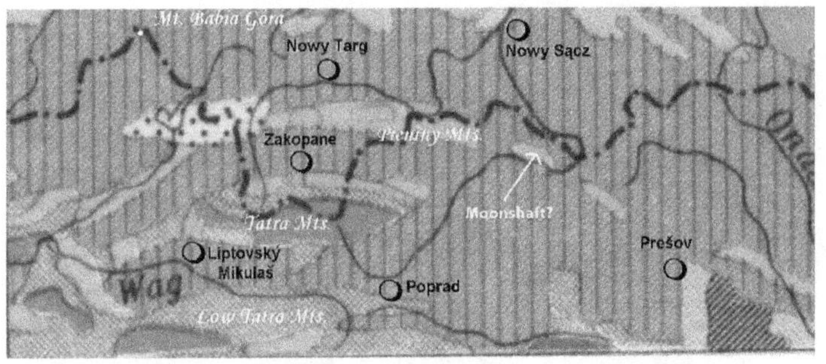

020 – Geological map of the Polish-Slovakian border. Rocky structures described by Dr. Horak appear in the place near the Sulin village, and also in the Pieniny Mts., High Tatra and Low Tatra Mts.

001	002		
003	003		
etc	Etc	till	020

ABOUT AUTHORS

ROBERT K. LEŚNIAKIEWICZ	**Dr. MILOŠ JESENSKÝ**

Robert Konstanty Leśniakiewicz (born on June 7, 1956 in Szamotuły) - Polish writer, translator and publicist, ufologist and researcher of other phenomena from the so-called "Borderline knowledge", also deals with environmental protection. A graduate of the Officer's Mechanized Forces Academy in Wroclaw. Reserve captain of the Forces of the Border Protection (1975–1991) and the Border Guard (1991–1994), civil specialty - forestry, forest protection. He currently lives in Jordanów.

From 1987, a member of the Space Contact Club and the Center for Research on Anomalous Phenomena in Krakow and a correspondent member of the Brazilian Centro Brasiliero de Pesquisas de Discos Voladores (since 2007), as well as the vice president of the Jordan Land Lovers Society in Jordanów, a member of the Mushroom Lovers Club, founding member and member (until 2010) of the board of the Mushroom Lovers Association in Krakow.

As part of his literary activity, he collaborated with the monthly magazines: Granica (1987–1991), Sfinks (1989–1991), the UFO quarterly (1990–1998), the monthly magazines Eko Świat (since 1994) and Nieznany Świat (since 1991) - and co-edited (together with Bronisław Rzepecki) the quarterly Peripheral Visions, UFO Time and World UFO (1997–2000), for which he wrote over 2000 articles and translations from English, Russian, Czech, Slovak and Swedish. He also co-edits the regional quarterly "Echo Jordanowa". He collaborated with Andrzej Zalewski as part of the Ekoradio broadcast of Program I of Polish Radio. He is the author and co-author of 31 books and translations from five languages, and runs two blogs devoted to UFOs and paleo-astronautics, ecology and other paranormal phenomena.

Dr Miloš Jesenský Ph.D. (born on May 23, 1973 in Čadca) is a Slovak researcher of anomalous phenomena, ufologist, writer and publicist. He studied at the University of Veterinary Medicine in Košice until 1995, then until 1999 he worked as an independent employee of the History Department at the East Slovakia Museum in Košice. From 1998, he was an independent researcher at the Faculty of History of the Slovak Academy of Sciences (SAV) in Bratislava. His doctoral thesis was entitled History of Alchemy in Slovakia, in the years 2001–2006 he worked in the Žilina Library as a bibliographic specialist, and then in the Office of Information and Foreign Contacts in the local government of the Žilina Region. Currently, he is the director of the Kysuce Museum in Čadca.

Dr Jesenský specializes in journalism in the field of history riddles, both in Slovakia and abroad. His literary output is extremely rich, he has written over 40 books, and his articles are published on websites and in magazines, also in Poland. He is a member of the Association of Slovak Writers and the Slovak Pen Club as well as the Syndicate of Slovak Journalists. He is also the winner of the Crystal Tiger Award (1998).

The sequel to *The Mooncave Mystery*, entitled *Return to Mooncave*, coming soon.

www.ingramcontent.com/pod-product-compliance
Lightning Source LLC
Chambersburg PA
CBHW030826270326
41928CB00007B/924
* 9 7 8 1 7 3 4 2 8 5 7 8 9 *